LARSON, BOSWELL, KANOLD, STIFF

Passport
to Mathematics

BOOK 2

Practice Workbook
Teacher's Edition
by David C. Falvo

Practice Workbook includes additional practice and problem solving exercises for each chapter lesson.

McDougal Littell
A HOUGHTON MIFFLIN COMPANY
Evanston, Illinois • Boston • Dallas

ISBN: 0-395-90159-6

3456789-PBO-02 01 00 99

Practice   1.1

Name _____

1. What happens to the area of a rectangle when its length and width are
   doubled? Tripled? Quadrupled? Complete the table showing the width,
   length, and area of the given rectangle. Describe the pattern of the
   areas. Check the pattern that you described by making a table for
   another rectangle. Does your pattern check?

	Width	Length	Area
Original	2	3	
Doubled			
Tripled			
Quadrupled			

2. You receive $25 for your birthday from your Grandparents. You go to
   the mall to buy 2 CD's that cost $10.95 and $12.95. Excluding tax, do
   you have enough money to buy both CD's? Explain your reasoning.

3. You are planning to bake a cake in home economics class. Your
   teacher tells you that you must first decide the flavor of cake mix and
   the color of the frosting before you actually start. You can choose
   from white, chocolate, or yellow cake and white, chocolate, or lemon
   frosting. How many different choices are possible? Make a list of the
   different cakes.

4. You go to a wholesale grocery store to buy some assorted bulk candy.
   One type costs $2.50 for 5 pounds and another type costs $3.50 for 6
   pounds. Which is the better bargain? Explain your reasoning.

In Exercises 1 and 2, find the missing number in the pattern. Explain your reasoning.

1. 5, 11, 17, 23, ?, 35

2. 2, 4, 8, 14, ?, 32

3. Count the number of dots in each array below. The number of dots is a square number. Complete the table below using the figures and the pattern for triangular numbers that you discovered in your text.

n = 1   n = 2   n = 3   n = 4   n = 5

Number	1	2	3	4	5
Triangular					
Square					

Determine a pattern for finding square numbers. Then determine a pattern to find square numbers using triangular numbers. Then find the 20th square number, using both patterns. Are your results the same? Explain.

4. Find the number of triangles in the figure at the right. Then describe your problem-solving strategy.

5. A 7th grade class has an enrollment of 20 girls and 18 boys. They are required to take ballroom dance lessons for physical education class. How many different girl-boy pairs are possible? Then describe your problem-solving strategy.

<table>
<tr><td>

Practice

</td><td>

1.3

</td><td>

Name _____

</td></tr>
</table>

In Exercises 1–4, use dot paper to sketch two similar figures of the given shape. Explain how you did it.

1. Triangle   **2.** Rectangle   **3.** Parallelogram   **4.** Hexagon

In Exercises 5–8, find the perimeter and area of the figure.

5.
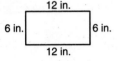

6.

7.
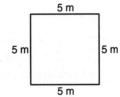

8.
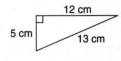

In Exercises 9–11, find the perimeter and area of the figure.

9.
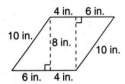

10.
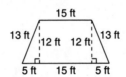

11.
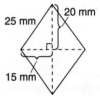

In Exercises 12–15, are the objects similar?

12. A basketball and a tennis ball   **13.** A pair of mittens

14. A guitar and a banjo   **15.** A protractor and a compass

In Exercises 16–18, show how four copies of the figure can be used to form a similar figure. Find the area. (The dots are one unit apart.)

16.
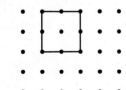

17.
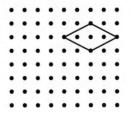

18.
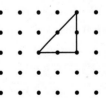

1. Mo and Vicki have been married for 10 years. They have 2 children, both boys. Out of 100 couples that have 2 children, estimate how many have exactly 2 boys? Construct a table and record the results of tossing a coin 2 times. Let heads represent a boy and tails represent a girl. Perform this experiment 100 times. Use your results to answer the question. Explain your results.

2. Maria has 2 brothers and 2 stepsisters and a stepbrother. There are 6 children in Maria's family. Instead of everyone buying everyone else a Christmas present, they pull names out of a hat, and then only buy that person a present. How many years would you expect it to take to pull the same name out of the hat? Describe and do a simulation to answer the question.

3. A cereal company has announced a contest in which it is giving away a mountain bike. To win the bike you must collect the letters "YOU WIN". There is one letter in each of the specially marked boxes of the cereal. You have the same chance of getting each letter. Describe and do a simulation to find the number of boxes that you would expect to have to buy to collect all 6 letters?

4. It is a hot and humid August afternoon. You have been at the beach all day and boy are you thirsty! You have found a soda machine. In the very bottom of your backpack you know that there are 4 quarters, 4 Susan B. Anthony dollars, and 4 Canadian quarters. The soda costs $0.50 and the machine will not accept Canadian quarters or give change. Estimate the number of times that it will take to pull 2 quarters out of your backpack when you pull 2 coins out. Describe and do a simulation that could be used to check your solution.

Name _____

In Exercises 1–3, complete the magic square so that each number is used once and the sum of the numbers along each row, column, and diagonal is the same.

1. Use numbers 1–9.

8		4
	5	
	7	

2. Use numbers 1–9.

2		6
4	3	

3. Use numbers 0–8.

5		7
	4	
	8	

In Exercises 4–6, use a calculator to find the value of _m_.

4. $m \times m = 441$

5. $m \times m = 961$

6. $m \times m = 2704$

In Exercises 7 and 8, use any strategy to find the number.

7. When you add me to 100, you get 6 times my value. What number am I?

8. When you subtract me from 160, you get 3 times my value. What number am I?

In Exercises 9–11, use the Guess, Check, and Revise strategy to solve the problem.

9. The sum of the scores on 3 History quizzes is 56. One score is 20. The other 2 scores are the same. What are they?

10. Sue is 4 times as old as her daughter Rachel. In 5 years Sue will only be 3 times as old as Rachel. How old are Sue and Rachel?

11. My grandfather was x years old in the year x^2. In what year was he born?

In Exercises 1–6, check the given value of the variable in the equation. Is it a solution?

1. $w + 5 = 24$, $w = 19$

2. $39 - d = 11$, $d = 28$

3. $5 \times t = 75$, $t = 25$

4. $\dfrac{m}{6} = 11$, $m = 66$

5. $12 + f = 51$, $f = 29$

6. $j - 13 = 16$, $j = 29$

In Exercises 7–12, solve the equation. Then check your solution.

7. $c + 5 = 25$

8. $\dfrac{g}{3} = 4$

9. $a - 15 = 2$

10. $6 \times q = 48$

11. $\dfrac{28}{b} = 4$

12. $y \times 12 = 48$

In Exercises 13–16, write an equation for each question. Then solve the equation to answer the question.

13. What number can be added to 12 to get 36?

14. What number can be subtracted from 26 to get 12?

15. What number can be multiplied by 7 to get 49?

16. What number can be divided by 11 to get 4?

In Exercises 17–19, solve the equation.

17. $8.25 + y = 12.56$

18. $\dfrac{9.1}{p} = 3.5$

19. $4.4 \times d = 23.1$

20. You and 3 friends go out for pizza. You divide a "King Kong" size pizza. There are 52 pieces of pizza in a "King Kong." Use the verbal model below. Assign labels and write an equation for this problem. Then solve the equation to find the number of pieces of pizza each of you get to eat.

$$\frac{\boxed{\text{Total number pieces of pizza}}}{\boxed{\text{Number of pieces per person}}} = \boxed{\text{Number of people in the group}}$$

1.7

Name _____

In Exercises 1–3, classify the following figures by writing the letters A through H in the Venn diagrams.

A.   B.   C.   D.

E.   F.   G.   H.

1. 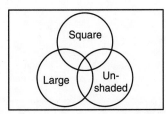   **2.** 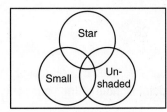   **3.**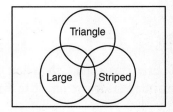

4. Mary, Larry, Harry, and Sherry are all brothers and sisters, in the Berry family.

* Harry is older than Sherry and Larry.

* Harry is younger than Mary.

* Larry is older than Sherry.

Order the children from oldest to youngest in the Berry family.

5. The favorite football teams of Brett, Gabrielle, Sue, and Jose are the 49ers, the Panthers, the Bengals, and the Cowboys. Each person has their own favorite team.

* Brett and Sue don't like the Panthers or the Cowboys.

* Gabrielle doesn't like the Panthers or the 49ers.

* Sue's favorite team's mascot is a member of the cat family.

Find each person's favorite team.

6. A survey asked the question, "What type of pet do you have, a dog or a cat?" Out of 100 children surveyed, 62 said that they have a dog, 42 said that they have a cat, and 24 said they have neither a dog nor a cat. How many children said that have both a dog and a cat? Illustrate your answer with a Venn diagram.

1. How many different combinations of at most 4 even numbers have a sum of 12?

2. Maria, Pierre, and Jackelyn are all running for class office. The student who receives the most votes is elected President. The student with the second highest number of votes is elected Vice-President, and the student with the third highest number of votes is elected secretary/Treasurer. How many different ways could these three positions be filled? List them.

In Exercises 3 and 4, show how the figure can be traced by going over each line exactly once and returning to the starting point without lifting your pencil.

3.

4.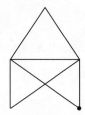

5. You want to buy a can of fruit juice from a vending machine but you have no change. The juice costs $0.65, and luckily the machine has a dollar bill slot. You insert a dollar bill and the machine drops your change. How many different ways could you receive your change, if the machine accepts only quarters, dimes and nickels? List them.

6. Trace the maze on a piece of paper. Is there more than one way for the monkey to get to the banana? If so, how many ways can you find?

7. Over the weekend, you went fishing and bought bait at the local bait and tackle shop. The shop was selling 1 dozen minnows for $2 and 1 dozen night crawlers for $1.00. If you spent $9, how many different ways could you have purchased bait? List them.

Name _____

In Exercises 1–3, solve the problem. Then tell what strategy or strategies you used.

1. Ginger collects stuffed animals. When she was 6 years old, she had twice as many stuffed animals as she did when she was 4 years old. At the age of 8 years, Ginger had 6 more than she did when she was 6. Now at the age of 12 years, she has 3 times as many stuffed animals as she did when she was 8. If she now has 60 different stuffed animals, how many did she have when she was 4 years old?

2. Derrick has a teen-age sister. If you add 10 years to her age, the number would be 4 times Derrick's age now. If you subtract 2 years from her age, the number would be 2 times Derrick's age now. What is Derrick's age?

3. Your school offers all natural light lunch in your school cafeteria. It consists of a salad and a bowl of fruit. There are 4 different types of salad and 6 different types of fruit from which to choose. How many different light lunches could you order without having the exact same lunch?

4. The bar graph shows the number of endangered animals in the United States, classified into different species as of 1996. Find the difference between the highest number of endangered species and the second highest number of endangered species. *(Source: Universal Almanac, 1997)*

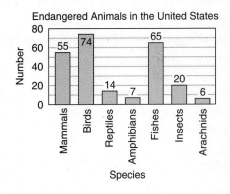
Endangered Animals in the United States

5. The bar graph shows the number of hospitals in the United States for the years 1960–1994. Describe the change in the number of hospitals during these years. What is your opinion of the reason that the number of hospitals is changing? *(Source: Universal Almanac, 1997)*

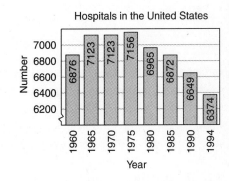
Hospitals in the United States

In Exercises 1 and 2, describe and correct the error.

1. $16 - 4 \div 2 = \dfrac{12}{2}$

$= 6$

2. $15 \div 3 + 2 = \dfrac{15}{5}$

$= 3$

In Exercises 3–11, evaluate the expression.

3. $9 - 3 \times 2$

4. $15 + 6 \div 3$

5. $6 \times 3 + 2$

6. $5 + 4 \div 2 - 3$

7. $22 - 10 \times 2 - 1$

8. $16 \div 4 + 10 \times 2$

9. $20 - 3(2 + 4)$

10. $(5 - 3) \times (8 + 1)$

11. $18 - (10 + 2) \div 4$

In Exercises 12–17, is the statement true or false? If it is false, insert parenthesis to make it true.

12. $14 \div 7 - 5 = 7$

13. $12 - 4 \div 2 = 10$

14. $25 + 15 \div 5 = 8$

15. $24 - 4 \times 2 + 2 = 8$

16. $8 \div 4 + 4 \times 6 = 26$

17. $10 \times 8 \div 2 + 6 = 10$

In Exercises 18–21, write the expression representing the following statement. Then evaluate the expression using a calculator.

18. 15 times 6 minus 25

19. 21 plus 144 divided by 16

20. 12.5 divided by 2 minus 5

21. 30.5 times 2 plus 3.4

Practice

2.2

Name _____

In Exercises 1–3, write the product as a power.

1. $4 \times 4 \times 4 \times 4 \times 4$

2. $d \cdot d \cdot d \cdot d$

3. $(e)(e)(e)(e)(e)(e)$

In Exercises 4–12, evaluate the expression.

4. 2^3

5. 10^3

6. 4^2

7. 3 squared

8. 5 cubed

9. 1^{14}

10. 2 to the fourth power

11. 4 to the third power

12. 8 to the second power

In Exercises 13–15, write an expression for the volume of the figure.

13.

14.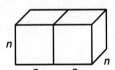

15.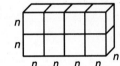

In Exercises 16–21, evaluate the expression when $w = 2$ and when $w = 5$.

16. $10 + w^3$

17. $w^3 - w^2$

18. $2 + w^2 \times 2$

19. $(w^2 - 1) \times (w^2 + 1)$

20. $(3 + w)^2$

21. $\dfrac{(6 - w)^2}{2}$

In Exercises 22–27, complete the statement using >, <, or =.

22. 2^5 ⬚ 5^2

23. 4^3 ⬚ 8^2

24. 3^4 ⬚ 2^6

25. 2^5 ⬚ 6^2

26. 5^4 ⬚ 25^2

27. 4^4 ⬚ 2^8

Name _____

In Exercises 1–3, complete the statement using *sometimes, always,* or *never.*
Give examples to support your answer.

1. A number that is divisible by 8 is _____ divisible by 2?

2. A number that is divisible by 5 is _____ divisible by 2?

3. A number that is divisible by 9 is divisible by 6?

In Exercises 4–11, use the divisibility tests to decide whether the number is
divisible by 2, 3, 4, 5, 6, 9, and 10.

4. 315   5. 600   6. 852   7. 1024

8. 8505   9. 6360   10. 12,548   11. 130,680

In Exercises 12–15, find all the digits that will make the number divisible by 9.

12. 4 ? 1   13. 15 ? 4   14. 2 ? ,456   15. 489,21 ?

In Exercises 16–19, sketch all the different sizes of rectangles with whole
number dimensions that have the given area.

16. 24 square units   17. 56 square units   18. 64 square units   19. 96 square units

20. Leap years occur every 4 years. 1992 was a leap year, and 1996 will
also be a leap year. Find a test that you can use to determine whether
any given year is a leap year. Then use your test to determine whether
the following years were or will be leap years.

a. 1492   b. 1776   c. 2000   d. 1902   e. 2042   f. 1964

Practice

2.4

Name _____

In Exercises 1–3, use a tree diagram to write the prime factorization of the number.

1. 36   **2.** 72   **3.** 180

In Exercises 4–6, use a calculator and divisibility tests to write the prime factorization of the number.

4. 2016   **5.** 1400   **6.** 10,800

In Exercises 7–12, find the number with the given prime factorization.

7. $2 \cdot 5^2$ **8.** $2 \cdot 3 \cdot 7$ **9.** $2^2 \cdot 3^3$

10. $2^2 \cdot 3^2 \cdot 5$ **11.** $2^3 \cdot 5^2$ **12.** $2^2 \cdot 3^2 \cdot 5 \cdot 7$

In Exercises 13–15, evaluate $2x + 5y$ for the given values of x and y. Then decide whether the number is prime or composite.

13. $x = 4, y = 3$ **14.** $x = 2, y = 5$ **15.** $x = 3, y = 3$

In Exercises 16 and 17, solve the number riddle.

16. I am a composite number between 20 and 30. The sum of my prime factors is the greatest of all the composites between 20 and 30. What number am I?

17. I am a prime number between 40 and 50. If you add one to me, the sum of the prime factors of that composite number is 11. What number am I?

18. A book called The Penguin Dictionary of Curious and Interesting Numbers by David Wells (1986) contains fascinating numbers and their properties. One of which is the only 3-digit numbers that are prime and all rearrangements of their digits are also prime are 113, 199, and 337. Find all 2-digit numbers that also have this property.

In Exercises 1–4, match the pair of numbers with their greatest common factor.

a. 3   **b.** 32   **c.** 6   **d.** 8

1. 18, 24   **2.** 45, 84   **3.** 24, 56   **4.** 64, 96

In Exercises 5–8, find the greatest common factor by listing all the factors of each number.

5. 15, 27   **6.** 12, 42   **7.** 45, 63   **8.** 48, 64

In Exercises 9–12, find a pair of numbers that have the given greatest common factor. Tell how you found the pair.

9. 4   **10.** 6   **11.** 9   **12.** 15

In Exercises 13–15, find the greatest common factor of the 3 numbers.

13. 12, 30, 48   **14.** 15, 40, 65   **15.** 24, 48, 72

16. You are cutting the small square patches to use to make a quilt. The size of the quilt is 60 inches by 72 inches. Find all the different size square patches that could be used. How many patches do you need of the different sizes to complete the entire quilt. What size of squares require the least amount of patches?

Practice 2.6

In Exercises 1–4, find a denominator for the fraction so that the greatest common factor of the numerator and the denominator is 4.

1. $\frac{8}{?}$

2. $\frac{12}{?}$

3. $\frac{20}{?}$

4. $\frac{36}{?}$

In Exercises 5–10, write the fraction in simplest form.

5. $\frac{30}{36}$

6. $\frac{24}{48}$

7. $\frac{15}{60}$

8. $\frac{18}{27}$

9. $\frac{48}{120}$

10. $\frac{60}{108}$

In Exercises 11–14, which 3 fractions are equivalent?

11. $\frac{3}{5}, \frac{9}{25}, \frac{15}{25}, \frac{18}{30}$

12. $\frac{45}{63}, \frac{10}{14}, \frac{5}{7}, \frac{25}{49}$

13. $\frac{28}{32}, \frac{14}{16}, \frac{21}{24}, \frac{35}{45}$

14. $\frac{4}{9}, \frac{16}{24}, \frac{20}{30}, \frac{2}{3}$

In Exercises 15–17, write 3 other fractions that equivalent to the given fraction. Include the simplest form of the fraction.

15. $\frac{16}{100}$

16. $\frac{32}{48}$

17. $\frac{21}{28}$

In Exercises 18–24, use the table. It shows the results of a survey that asked 200 middle school students, "What is your favorite summer time activity?" Write the responses as a fraction of the total surveyed in simplest terms.

18. Bicycling

19. Swimming

20. Movies

21. Mall

22. Sports

23. In-line skating

24. Camping

Response	Number of children
Bicycling	30
Going swimming	36
Going to the movies	20
Hanging out at the mall	25
Playing organized sports	55
In-line skating/roller-skating	18
Camping	16

In Exercises 1–4, write the fraction as an equivalent fraction with a denominator of 100. Then write the equivalent decimal.

1. $\frac{3}{4}$

2. $\frac{4}{5}$

3. $\frac{16}{25}$

4. $\frac{11}{20}$

In Exercises 5–8, write the fraction as a decimal. Round your answer to the nearest hundredth.

5. $\frac{5}{8}$

6. $\frac{1}{6}$

7. $\frac{7}{12}$

8. $\frac{1}{3}$

In Exercises 9–12, use a calculator to write the fraction as a decimal. Round your answer to the nearest hundredth.

9. $\frac{11}{25}$

10. $\frac{12}{55}$

11. $\frac{18}{35}$

12. $\frac{17}{36}$

In Exercises 13 and 14, write the fractions as decimals using a bar to show any repeating decimals. Describe any pattern that you see.

13. $\frac{4}{33} = ?, \frac{5}{33} = ?, \frac{6}{33} = ?$

14. $\frac{27}{99} = ?, \frac{28}{99} = ?, \frac{29}{99} = ?$

In Exercises 15–18, write each decimal as a fraction with a numerator of 1.

15. 0.01

16. 0.5

17. $0.\overline{1}$

18. 0.02

In Exercises 19–24, use the following. According to the U.S. Bureau of the Census, 75 of every 100 persons in the world live in only 22 countries. The other 25 live in any one of the remaining 184 countries. For each country listed write the fraction and the decimal of the number of people out of 100 that live in that country. *(Source: Universal Almanac, 1995)*

19. China   21

20. India   16

21. Former Soviet Union   5

22. United States   5

23. Indonesia   4

24. Japan   2

In Exercises 1 and 2, estimate the values of *a* and *b* on the real number line.
Then use > or < to write a statement that relates the values.

1.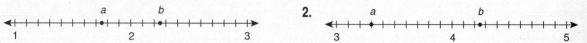

2.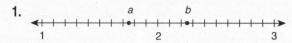

In Exercises 3–6, plot the numbers on a real number line. Then order the numbers
from least to greatest.

3. 2.5, 4.25, 3.05, 4.75, 3.45, 3.95

4. $\frac{4}{5}, \frac{7}{8}, \frac{1}{2}, \frac{2}{5}, \frac{8}{5}, \frac{9}{4}$

5. $\frac{15}{6}, \frac{12}{7}, \frac{16}{9}$, 1.75, 2.25, $\frac{18}{5}$

6. $\frac{25}{3}, \frac{36}{5}, \frac{49}{8}, \frac{25}{4}$, 6.4, $\frac{80}{9}$

In Exercises 7 and 8, plot the numbers on a number line. Describe the pattern
and write the next 2 numbers.

7. $\frac{1}{4}$, 0.65, $\frac{21}{20}$, 1.45, $\frac{37}{20}$

8. $\frac{13}{5}$, 3.1, $\frac{18}{5}$, $\frac{41}{10}$, $\frac{23}{5}$

9. Order the numbers to unscramble the words.

F	I	T	S	M	U	H	A	N
$\frac{10}{3}$	$\frac{9}{4}$	$\frac{16}{9}$	$\frac{8}{3}$	$\frac{2}{3}$	3.4	$\frac{41}{20}$	1.25	3.75

10. Use a time line to organize the dates in the chronology of United States
history.

 * 1804   Lewis and Clark Expedition sets out from St. Louis.
 * 1929   Stock Market crashes on "Black Tuesday," October 29.
 * 1775   American Revolution begins with Battle of Lexington and Concord, April 19.
 * 1861   Civil War begins with attack on Fort Sumter, April 12.
 * 1917   Congress declares war on Germany and Hungary bringing U.S. into World War I.
 * 1990   U.S. launches Operation Desert Shield.
 * 1963   Martin Luther King delivers his "I Have a Dream" speech, August 28.
 * 1945   U. S. drops atomic bombs on Hiroshima and Nagasaki ending World War II.

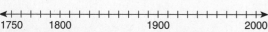

In Exercises 1–6, list the first 10 multiples of each number. Then find the least common multiple.

1. 3, 10 **2.** 2, 9 **3.** 4, 18

4. 12, 16 **5.** 2, 3, 6 **6 .** 3, 4, 8

In Exercises 7–12, find the least common multiple of the numbers.

7. 24, 32 **8.** 45, 105 **9.** 48, 144

10. 90, 198 **11.** 2, 5, 7 **12.** 3, 4, 5

In Exercises 13–15, find the values of $2 \cdot n$ and $3 \cdot n$. Then find the least common multiple of the two values.

13. $n = 5$ **14.** $n = 6$ **15.** $n = 7$

16. Ginger and Sue both work at the community pool as lifeguards during the summer. The pool opens for the summer on May 1. The pool is open 7 days a week until September 30. Ginger has every 8th day off, and Sue has every 6th day off. Will Ginger and Sue have any days off together during the summer? If so, what are the dates?

Practice	3.2	Name _____

In Exercises 1–4, is the fraction proper or improper? Explain.

1. $\frac{7}{9}$ 2. $\frac{12}{7}$ 3. $\frac{8}{3}$ 4. $\frac{15}{16}$

In Exercises 5–8, match the number with its equivalent fraction or decimal.

a. 3.6   b. $\frac{17}{5}$ c. 4.2   d. $4\frac{1}{2}$

5. 3.4   6. $\frac{21}{5}$ 7. $\frac{9}{2}$ 8. $3\frac{3}{5}$

In Exercises 9–12, rewrite the improper fraction as a mixed number.

9. $\frac{13}{2}$ 10. $\frac{19}{7}$ 11. $\frac{26}{8}$ 12. $\frac{39}{5}$

In Exercises 13–16, rewrite the mixed number as an improper fraction.

13. $1\frac{7}{8}$ 14. $2\frac{5}{11}$ 15. $8\frac{5}{9}$ 16. $12\frac{1}{3}$

In Exercises 17–20, rewrite the improper fraction as a decimal.

17. $\frac{18}{5}$ 18. $\frac{25}{4}$ 19. $\frac{37}{10}$ 20. $\frac{28}{5}$

In Exercises 21–24, rewrite the mixed number as a decimal.

21. $1\frac{7}{8}$ 22. $3\frac{7}{16}$ 23. $5\frac{3}{20}$ 24. $4\frac{9}{25}$

In Exercises 25 and 26, is the statement true or false? If false, change it to a true statement.

25. Two and four sevenths is equal to eighteen sevenths.

26. Four and two tenths is equal to twenty-two tenths.

In Exercises 1–8, add or subtract. Simplify if possible.

1. $\frac{3}{5} + \frac{1}{5}$

2. $\frac{9}{11} - \frac{7}{11}$

3. $\frac{4}{5} + \frac{2}{3}$

4. $\frac{2}{7} + \frac{1}{3}$

5. $\frac{8}{9} - \frac{1}{5}$

6. $\frac{7}{10} - \frac{2}{3}$

7. $\frac{1}{2} + \frac{2}{3} + \frac{1}{6}$

8. $\frac{3}{8} + \frac{1}{6} + \frac{5}{12}$

In Exercises 9–11, find the sums or differences. Then continue the pattern to find the next two sums or differences.

9. $\frac{1}{2} + \frac{1}{32}$

$\frac{1}{2} + \frac{1}{16}$

$\frac{1}{2} + \frac{1}{8}$

10. $\frac{1}{7} + \frac{1}{2}$

$\frac{2}{7} + \frac{1}{2}$

$\frac{3}{7} + \frac{1}{2}$

11. $\frac{1}{4} - \frac{1}{24}$

$\frac{1}{4} - \frac{1}{20}$

$\frac{1}{4} - \frac{1}{16}$

In Exercises 12–17, use mental math or the Guess, Check, and Revise strategy to find the missing fraction in simplest form.

12. $? + \frac{2}{5} = 1$

13. $\frac{8}{11} - ? = \frac{2}{11}$

14. $\frac{1}{2} + ? = \frac{5}{6}$

15. $? + \frac{3}{8} = \frac{3}{4}$

16. $? - \frac{1}{4} = \frac{1}{3}$

17. $\frac{1}{5} + ? = \frac{1}{2}$

18. Jerri and Joseph are twin brothers. Jerri weighed $8\frac{3}{4}$ pounds when he was born, and Joseph weighed $8\frac{11}{16}$ pounds. Which brother weighed more? How much more?

19. For physical education class you had to run for 15 minutes and the distance was recorded. You ran $1\frac{2}{5}$ miles and your friend ran $1\frac{3}{8}$ miles. Who ran further? How much further?

In Exercises 1–4, simplify the mixed number.

1. $3\frac{7}{5}$ **2.** $6\frac{8}{12}$ **3.** $2\frac{15}{12}$ **4.** $10\frac{24}{18}$

In Exercises 5–8, add or subtract. Simplify if possible.

5. $\begin{aligned}5\frac{1}{9}\\+\ 2\frac{5}{9}\end{aligned}$ **6.** $\begin{aligned}4\frac{3}{8}\\+\ 6\frac{1}{4}\end{aligned}$ **7.** $\begin{aligned}6\frac{2}{7}\\-\ 4\frac{6}{7}\end{aligned}$ **8.** $\begin{aligned}4\frac{1}{5}\\-\ 1\frac{7}{10}\end{aligned}$

In Exercises 9–12, find the difference. Simplify if possible.

9. $8\frac{5}{12} - 2\frac{5}{6}$ **10.** $8\frac{2}{3} - 6\frac{1}{5}$ **11.** $10 - 2\frac{7}{16}$ **12.** $12\frac{1}{6} - 10\frac{3}{4}$

In Exercises 13–15, how much of the given fencing will be left over when you fence the yard to keep Sparky from running away?

13. Fencing: 50 feet

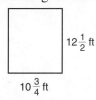

$12\frac{1}{2}$ ft

$10\frac{3}{4}$ ft

14. Fencing: 40 yards

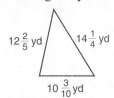

$12\frac{2}{5}$ yd $14\frac{1}{4}$ yd

$10\frac{3}{10}$ yd

15. Fencing: 100 feet

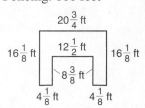

$20\frac{3}{4}$ ft

$16\frac{1}{8}$ ft $12\frac{1}{2}$ ft $16\frac{1}{8}$ ft

$8\frac{3}{8}$ ft

$4\frac{1}{8}$ ft $4\frac{1}{8}$ ft

16. For an economic's class project you were to pick one stock from the newspaper and follow its progress for a week. The stock you chose had a value of $48\frac{1}{2}$ on Monday morning. The table gives the change in value for that day. Find the stock's value at the end of each day.

Monday	Tuesday	Wednesday	Thursday	Friday
Up $\frac{7}{8}$	Down $\frac{3}{4}$	Up $\frac{1}{8}$	Up $\frac{3}{8}$	Down $\frac{1}{4}$

In Exercises 1–12, multiply. Simplify if possible.

1. $\frac{2}{3} \times \frac{6}{7}$

2. $\frac{5}{6} \cdot \frac{9}{10}$

3. $\frac{2}{7}$ of 21

4. $12 \times \frac{7}{8}$

5. $1\frac{4}{5} \cdot 4\frac{1}{3}$

6. $3\frac{1}{5}$ of $6\frac{1}{4}$

7. $\frac{4}{9} \times 5\frac{1}{8}$

8. $5\frac{1}{4} \cdot \frac{2}{3}$

9. $1\frac{1}{4}$ of $10\frac{3}{4}$

10. $8 \cdot 2\frac{3}{4}$

11. $\frac{1}{6} \cdot \frac{3}{4} \cdot 2\frac{5}{6}$

12. $8 \times \frac{11}{16} \times 5\frac{1}{2}$

In Exercises 13–15, find the area of the region.

13.

14.

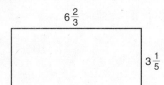

15.

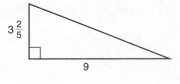

16. Your favorite recipe for chocolate fudge nut cookies calls for $3\frac{3}{4}$ cups of sugar. The recipe is designed to make only 1 dozen cookies. If you needed to make 64 cookies, which is $5\frac{1}{3}$ dozen, how many cups of sugar do you need?

17. The following table gives the number of laps that a high school swim team swam in a week. A complete lap is $\frac{2}{5}$ of a mile. Determine the total number of laps and the distance the team has swum.

Monday	Tuesday	Wednesday	Thursday	Friday
$2\frac{1}{2}$	$2\frac{1}{4}$	$1\frac{3}{4}$	$2\frac{1}{4}$	$2\frac{1}{2}$

In Exercises 1 and 2, use the Distributive Property to write two expressions that are represented by the area model.

1.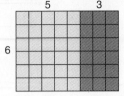

2.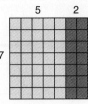

In Exercises 3–8, evaluate the expression.

3. $8(6 + 3)$

4. $12(10 + 4)$

5. $10(2.5 + 1.6)$

6. $4(\frac{1}{4} + \frac{5}{6})$

7. $6(\frac{1}{2} + \frac{3}{4})$

8. $9(\frac{2}{3} + \frac{7}{9})$

In Exercises 9–14, use the Distributive Property to rewrite the expression.

9. $8(t + 2)$

10. $14(4 + f)$

11. $d(3 + 8)$

12. $e(13 + 2)$

13. $2(f + p)$

14. $1(v + 9)$

In Exercises 15 and 16, evaluate the expressions when $y = 4$. What can you conclude?

15. $3(y + 7)$ and $3y + 21$

16. $5(\frac{7}{10} + y)$ and $5(\frac{7}{10}) + 5y$

In Exercises 17–20, complete the statement without using pencil and paper.

17. $6(10.5) = 6(10 + 0.5) = \boxed{?}$

18. $80(2.1) = 80(2 + 0.1) = \boxed{?}$

19. $4(50.8) = 4(50 + 0.8) = \boxed{?}$

20. $12(5.04) = 12(5 + 0.04) = \boxed{?}$

In Exercises 1–4, match the expression with its value.

a. $\frac{7}{18}$ b. 13   c. $1\frac{1}{2}$ d. $\frac{1}{13}$

1. $3\frac{1}{4} \div \frac{1}{4}$ **2.** $\frac{1}{4} \div 3\frac{1}{4}$ **3.** $1\frac{3}{4} \div 4\frac{1}{2}$ **4.** $4\frac{1}{2} \div 3$

In Exercises 5–16, divide. Simplify if possible.

5. $4\frac{5}{6} \div 1\frac{1}{2}$ **6.** $7\frac{1}{8} \div 3\frac{1}{3}$ **7.** $\frac{15}{16} \div 1\frac{2}{3}$ **8.** $8\frac{5}{6} \div 6\frac{4}{5}$

9. $2\frac{1}{2} \div \frac{5}{8}$ **10.** $4\frac{3}{7} \div 1\frac{3}{4}$ **11.** $10\frac{3}{5} \div 4\frac{1}{6}$ **12.** $1 \div 3\frac{7}{8}$

13. $4\frac{9}{10} \div 2$ **14.** $1\frac{5}{8} \div 1\frac{3}{10}$ **15.** $7\frac{1}{3} \div 4\frac{1}{2}$ **16.** $6\frac{11}{12} \div 4$

In Exercises 17–22, use mental math to solve the equation.

17. $\frac{2}{3} \div ? = 1$ **18.** $5 \div ? = 15$ **19.** $? \div 2 = \frac{1}{4}$

20. $? \div \frac{1}{5} = 10$ **21.** $\frac{1}{8} \div ? = \frac{5}{8}$ **22.** $\frac{7}{2} \div ? = \frac{21}{8}$

In Exercises 23 and 24, write the problem that is represented by the phrase.
Then solve the problem.

23. Five eighths *divided by* two and one fourth

24. Six and two thirds *divided by* three and five ninths

25. You are cutting material to make costumes for your school production
of "Phantom of the Opera." You have $56\frac{1}{2}$ feet of material and you need
to cut pieces that are $3\frac{1}{8}$ feet. How many full pieces can you cut?
Explain your reasoning.

Practice	4.1 Name _____

In Exercises 1–4, make a table of values. Use $x = 1, 2, 3, 4, 5$ and 6.

1. $2x + 3$ **2.** $x \div 2$ **3.** $5 + 8x$ **4.** $42 - 4x$

In Exercises 5–7, write an expression for the pattern. Then use the expression to make a table of values for $y = 1, 2, 3, 4$ and 5 that fits the pattern.

5. The value of the expression begins at 5 . Each time y increases by 1, the value of the expression increases by 6.

6. The value of the expression begins at 20. Each time y increases by 1, the value of the expression decreases by 2.

7. The value of the expression begins at 11. Each time y increases by 1, the value of the expression increases by 7.

8. You own a pizza shop. Make a table of values for ordering a pizza with 1, 2, 3, 4, and 5 toppings. Then write an expression that represents the cost of ordering a pizza with n toppings.

    a. A small pizza: $3, plus $1 per topping

    b. A large pizza: $8, plus $1.50 per topping

Practice

4.2

Name _____

In Exercises 1–6, write the ordered pair that is represented by the letter.

1. A

2. B

3. C

4. D

5. E

6. F

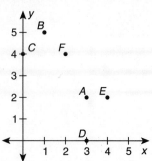

In Exercises 7 and 8, write the ordered pairs represented by the table.
Then draw a scatter plot of the data.

7.

x	1	2	3	4	5	6
y	1	3	5	7	9	11

8.

x	1	2	3	4	5	6
y	14	12	10	8	6	4

In Exercises 9 and 10, complete the table. Then draw a scatter plot of the data.
Describe any patterns in the scatter plot.

9.

x	1	2	3	4	5
y	5	7	9		

10.

x	1	2	3	4	5
y	15	12			3

11. Camp Waka-Waka charges $3 for 2 adults and $3 for each child. So the cost of 2 adults and x children is given by $y = 3 + 3x$. Camp Barking Spider charges $6 for 2 adults and $2 for each child. So the cost for 2 adults and x children is $y = 6 + 2x$. Complete the tables. Then draw a scatter plot for each table. Which camp would you go to? Explain.

Camp Waka-Waka

Children	1	2	3	4	5	6
Cost ($)						

Camp Barking Spider

Children	1	2	3	4	5	6
Cost ($)						

In Exercises 1–4, graph the numbers on a number line. Describe the pattern and find the missing integers.

1. –7, –4, –1, 2, 5, ?, ?

2. 12, 8, 4, 0, –4, ?, ?

3. 8, 7, 5, 2, –2, ?, ?

4. –10, –9, –6, –1, 6, ?, ?

In Exercises 5–8, complete the statement using < or >.

5. –9 ? 8

6. –5 ? –4

7. 8 ? –16

8. –15 ? –25

In Exercises 9–11, is the statement true or false? Support your answer with a number line drawing.

9. Negative two is less than negative five.

10. Negative twelve is greater than negative nine.

11. The distance from six to zero is greater than the distance from negative seven to zero.

In Exercises 12–17, write the number represented by the real-life situation.

12. 12 feet below sea level

13. An elevation of 2820 feet

14. The value of a stock fell $50

15. A twelve yard loss

16. A $500 deposit

17. A 2-point deduction

In Exercises 18–20, order the numbers from least to greatest.

18. –5, 4, –8, 2, 0

19. 1.25, –2.5, 1.02, –1, 0

20. $-\frac{7}{4}$, $-\frac{5}{2}$, 2.5, –4.5, –4.05

In Exercises 1 and 2, write the addition problem that is illustrated by the number line. Then solve the problem.

1.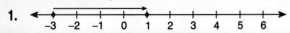

2.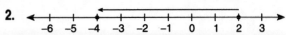

In Exercises 3–10, find the sum.

3. $4 + 2$ 4. $-9 + 5$ 5. $5 + (-3)$ 6. $-8 + (-2)$

7. $6 + (-3)$ 8. $-1 + (-3)$ 9. $-10 + 15$ 10. $-24 + (-15)$

In Exercises 11–13, match the addition problem with the keystrokes. Then solve the problem.

a. 5 $\boxed{+}$ 3 $\boxed{+/-}$ $\boxed{=}$ b. 5 $\boxed{+/-}$ $\boxed{+}$ 3 $\boxed{+/-}$ $\boxed{=}$ c. 5 $\boxed{+/-}$ $\boxed{+}$ 3 $\boxed{=}$

11. $-5 + (-3)$ 12. $-5 + 3$ 13. $5 + (-3)$

In Exercises 14–16, use a calculator to find the average.

14. $-23, 52, -35$ 15. $-85, 74, -25$ 16. $-25, 26, 15$

In Exercises 17–19, decide whether the expression $-4 + x$ is positive, negative, or zero.

17. x is greater than 5.   18. x is 4.   19. x is less than 3.

In Exercises 20–22, evaluate the expression when $y = -3$.

20. $-5 + y$ 21. $8 + y$ 22. $y + (-3)$

In Exercises 23 and 24, imagine that you are living in International Falls, Montana for the winter.

23. You wake up at 7 A.M. and the temperature is –6° F. By noon the temperature has risen 18 degrees. Write an addition problem you could use to determine the temperature at noon.

24. At midnight the temperature is –2° F. During the night the temperature drops 13 degrees. Write an addition problem you could use to determine the temperature the next morning.

Practice

4.5

Name _____

In Exercises 1 and 2, describe and correct the error in the number-line model.
Then solve the problem.

1. $5 - (-3)$

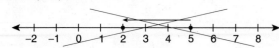

2. $-8 - 5$

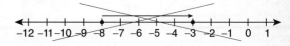

In Exercises 3–6, match the expression with its description.

a. Zero   **b. Positive**   **c. Negative**

3. $-2 - 2$ **4.** $2 - (-2)$ **5.** $-2 - (-2)$

In Exercises 6–8, use a number line to find the difference.

6. $-5 - (-1)$ **7.** $8 - (-2)$ **8.** $6 - (-5)$

In Exercises 9–17, find the difference.

9. $12 - (-2)$ **10.** $-5 - 8$ **11.** $-12 - (-10)$

12. $15 - (-15)$ **13.** $-8 - (-8)$ **14.** $-12 - 32$

15. $42 - (-10)$ **16.** $-49 - 1$ **17.** $64 - (-4)$

In Exercises 18–22, use a calculator to solve.

18. $-48 - 98$ **19.** $95 - (-82)$ **20.** $156 - (-464)$

21. $-215 - 584$ **22.** $-564 - (-546)$ **23.** $1032 - (-299)$

In Exercises 24 and 25, solve the number riddle.

24. I am an integer. I am less than zero. When you subtract me from −5 the
result is 0. What number am I?

25. I am an integer. The difference between myself and 10 is the same as
the difference between −6 and myself. What number am I?

In Exercises 1–9, solve the equation. Then check your solution.

1. $d + 4 = -9$ 2. $18 = t + 12$ 3. $15 + k = 10$

4. $z + 1.5 = -2.5$ 5. $j + 6.3 = 5.2$ 6. $w + \frac{7}{8} = \frac{3}{4}$

7. $\frac{5}{16} = s + \frac{1}{2}$ 8. $1.64 = y + 10.52$ 9. $p + 19 = -45$

In Exercises 10–12, write 3 different equations that have the given solution.

10. -5 11. -20 12. $-\frac{1}{8}$

In Exercises 13–16, write the equation that represents the statement. Then solve the equation.

13. The sum of a number and four is negative five.

14. The sum of twenty and a number is negative fifteen.

15. Negative two is the sum of eighteen and a number.

16. Sixteen is the sum of a number and thirteen.

In Exercises 17–22, use a calculator to solve the equation.

17. $e + 158 = -125$ 18. $-512 = f + 875$ 19. $m + 158.26 = 101.25$

20. $w + 0.025 = 0.01$ 21. $1058 = j + 999.5$ 22. $845.26 = 1011.06 + s$

23. On a very cold night in North Dakota the temperature reached a record low for that date. By morning the temperature had risen 15 degrees, but was still 8 degrees below zero. Write a verbal model, labels, and an equation to find the record low temperature the night before.

Practice 4.7

Name _____

In Exercises 1–3, without solving the equation, decide whether the solution is positive or negative. Then check your solution by solving the equation.

1. $15 + e = 10$

2. $-18 + r = -26$

3. $-19 = y + -28$

In Exercises 4–6, write an addition and a subtraction equation that have the given solution.

4. $d = -8$

5. $8 = r$

6. $w = -2$

In Exercises 7–18, solve the equation. Then check your solution.

7. $d - 9 = -10$

8. $-3 = t - 8$

9. $f - 14 = 18$

10. $s - 12 = -2$

11. $-12 = w + 18$

12. $z - 22 = -30$

13. $-24 = u - 30$

14. $q - \frac{1}{5} = \frac{1}{10}$

15. $-21 + i = 18$

16. $2\frac{1}{4} = e - 1\frac{2}{3}$

17. $g - 12.56 = 10.28$

18. $-20.5 = j - 10.65$

In Exercises 19–21, write the equation that is represented by the statement. Then solve the equation.

19. The difference of a number and twelve is negative twelve.

20. Thirty two is the sum of a number and fifty one.

21. Negative three eighths is the difference of a number and one sixth.

22. You stop at a convenience store to get something to eat. You order 2 hot dogs and a freezy. The hot dogs are on special, 2 for 99¢, and the freezy costs 79¢. The clerk gives you $3.22 in change, but you forgot how much you gave the clerk. Write a verbal model, labels, and an equation to determine how much money you gave the clerk.

In Exercises 1–4, order the data from least to greatest. Then find the mean, median and mode of the data.

1. Number of inches of snow that fell on 14 towns in a 50 mile radius during a snow storm: 8, 4, 7 ,6, 5, 6, 7, 8, 9, 10, 11, 5, 4,8

2. Cost of admission to a movie at 20 different cinemas:
$4.25, $3.75, $5.00, $5.25, $4.00, $4.50, $5.00, $3.75, $5.25, $6.25, $5.75, $6.00, $5.50, $5.75, $6.25, $6.50, $7.00, $6.25, $6.50, $6.25

3. Number of states 20 people have visited: 5, 15, 30, 18, 3, 14, 26, 7, 5, 4, 3, 2, 1, 44, 16, 14, 9, 10, 12, 3

4. Number of people living in 25 different households: 2, 3, 2, 5, 4, 6, 10, 5, 4, 3, 6, 5, 2, 3, 4, 9, 6, 4, 5, 2, 11, 8, 4, 4, 3

In Exercises 5 and 6, create a data set of 6 numbers with the given measures of central tendency.

5. Mean: 12, median: 12, mode: 10

6. Mean: 82, median: 80, mode: 82

7. The table shows the number of nations represented in the Winter Olympic Games from 1948 through 1994. Find the mean, median and mode of the data. Which do you think best represents the data? Explain.
(Source: Universal Almanac, 1997)

Year	Nations
1948	28
1952	30
1956	32
1960	30
1964	36
1968	37
1972	35
1976	37
1980	37
1984	49
1988	57
1992	64
1994	67

Practice 5.2

Name _____

In Exercises 1 and 2, use the histogram. It shows the number of single never married females (in thousands) in the United States by age group for 1994. *(Source: Universal Almanac, 1997)*

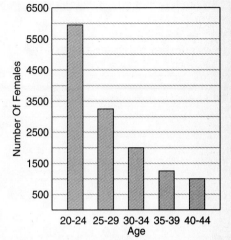

1. What age interval has the greatest number? What age interval has the least?

2. Write a summary statement about the number of single never married females in the United States in 1994.

3. The data below shows the approximate number of foreign born residents (in thousands) of each state in 1990. States with more than 600,000 foreign-born residents have been excluded from the table. Make a frequency table for this data. Then draw a histogram of the data. *(Source: Universal Almanac, 1997)*

AK	25	IA	43	MI	355	NM	81	TN	59
AL	44	ID	29	MN	113	NV	105	UT	59
AR	25	IN	94	MO	84	OH	260	VA	312
AZ	278	KS	63	MS	20	OK	65	VT	18
CO	142	KY	34	MT	14	OR	139	WA	322
CT	279	LA	87	NC	115	PA	369	WI	36
DE	22	MA	574	ND	9	RI	95	WV	16
GA	173	MD	313	NE	28	SC	50	WY	8
HI	163	ME	36	NH	41	SD	8		

4. The data shows the average cost per day (in dollars) of hospital care by state for 1990 and 1994, respectively. Make a histogram for the average cost per day of hospital care for 1990 and 1994. Use different colored bars for 1990 and 1994. *(Source: Universal Almanac, 1997)*

AK	534	724	HI	638	958	ME	574	802	NJ	613	934	SD	391	470
AL	588	781	IA	495	672	MI	716	929	NM	734	1047	TN	633	870
AR	534	724	ID	547	679	MN	536	695	NV	854	1016	TX	752	1055
AZ	867	1091	IL	717	988	MO	679	915	NY	641	854	UT	832	1115
CA	939	1301	IN	667	955	MS	439	583	OH	720	1008	VA	635	885
CO	725	993	KS	532	715	MT	405	470	OK	632	848	VT	598	651
CT	825	1121	KY	563	748	NC	595	806	OR	800	1077	WA	817	1206
DE	771	1042	LA	701	929	ND	427	515	PA	662	892	WI	554	802
FL	769	975	MA	788	1131	NE	490	606	RI	663	970	WV	565	727
GA	630	797	MD	678	981	NH	671	825	SC	590	876	WY	462	504

5.3

Name _____

In Exercises 1–4, match the data with the box-and-whisker plot.

a.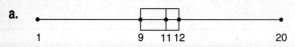

b.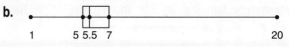

c.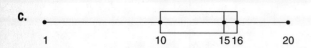

d.

1. 1, 10, 15, 18, 16, 14, 15, 16, 8, 20

2. 6, 2, 3, 8, 1, 2, 5, 6, 8, 20

3. 1, 12, 15, 8, 9, 10, 11, 12, 11, 20

4. 5, 8, 7, 6, 5, 4, 5, 6, 1, 20

In Exercises 5–7, draw a box-and-whisker plot of the data.

5. 3, 6, 5, 12, 14, 18, 18, 8, 9, 10, 12, 17, 18, 20

6. 18, 20, 28, 32, 34, 25, 12, 18, 19, 29, 30, 32, 36, 40

7. 84, 89, 92, 100, 102, 82, 64, 84, 77, 82, 78, 92, 94, 96, 80, 68

In Exercises 8 and 9, use the following data. It shows the age of the Presidents of the United States at the time of their inauguration. *(Source: Information Please Almanac, 1995)*

57, 61, 57, 57, 58, 57, 61, 54, 68, 51, 49, 64, 50, 48, 65, 52, 56, 46, 54, 49, 50, 47, 55, 55, 54, 42, 51, 56, 55, 54, 51, 54, 51, 60, 62, 43, 55, 56, 61, 52, 69, 64, 46

8. Make a box-and-whisker plot of the data.

9. What does the plot tell you about the age of the Presidents?

<table>
<tr><td>Practice</td><td>5.4</td><td>Name _____</td></tr>
</table>

In Exercises 1–4, plot the points in a coordinate plane.

1. (4, −2), (−1, 5), (0, 5), (−2, 0)

2. (3, 2), (−5, −1), (6, −3), (−4, −4)

3. (−3, 4), (−2, 1), (4, −5), (4, −4)

4. (1, 1), (−4, −2), (5, −4), (−3, 0)

In Exercises 5 and 6, use the scatter plot. It shows the daily high temperatures from January 21 to January 25 in a rural area of Montana.

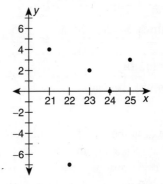

5. Explain what happened to the high temperature each day.

6. The high temperature on January 21st was 4° F. What was the next highest temperature?

7. The table below gives the average cost of a 4-year college including tuition and fees for years 1990–1996. The costs are in hundreds of dollars. Draw a scatter plot for the data. Describe any pattern you see in your scatter plot. *(Source: Universal Almanac, 1997)*

Year	1990	1991	1992	1993	1994	1995	1996
Cost	17.8	19.1	21.4	23.3	25.4	27.1	28.6

In Exercises 8–11, use the table. It shows the profits or losses your business had each month for one year. (Note: Positive numbers represent profits and negative numbers represent losses.)

8. Draw a scatter plot of the data.

9. Describe any patterns in your scatter plot.

Fast Food	Ice Cream
$300	−$200
$260	−$60
$220	$80
$180	$220
$140	$360
$100	$500
$133	$385
$167	$267
$200	$150
$234	$31
$267	−$85
$300	−$200

10. If your profit on fast food was $150 in a month, what would you expect your profit or your loss to be on ice cream?

11. If you had a $100 loss (−$100) on ice cream, what would you expect to get on fast food?

In Exercises 1–3, use a line graph or a bar graph to represent the data in the table. Describe any patterns you see.

1.

Time (minutes)	5	10	15	20	25	30
Amount (grams)	65	115	165	215	265	315

2.

Year	1990	1991	1992	1993	1994	1995
Value	$525	$500	$475	$450	$425	$400

3.

Time (days)	1	2	3	4	5	6
Weight (pounds)	24	18	16	12	6	2

4. The table below shows the number of livestock on farms in the United States in millions for 1995. Make a bar graph of the data. Describe any patterns you see. The number of chickens on farms in 1995 was 5384 million. How would that number fit into your bar graph? *(Source: The Information Please Almanac, 1997)*

Animal	Cattle	Dairy Cows	Sheep	Swine	Turkeys
Number	103	9	9	60	293

5. The table at the right shows the average hours of household TV usage in hours and minutes per day for the years 1988–1994. Draw a line graph of the data. Describe any patterns you see. (Note: The estimates are based on a 48 week average from September to August of the following year.) *(Source: The Information Please Almanac, 1997)*

Year	Time
1988	7 hr 2 min
1989	6 hr 55 min
1990	6 hr 56 min
1991	7 hr 4 min
1992	7 hr 17 min
1993	7 hr 21 min
1994	7 hr 20 min

6. The table at the right shows the top ten total number of medals awarded at the 1996 Summer Olympic Games in Atlanta, Georgia. Make a pictograph of the data. Describe any patterns that you see. *(Source: Universal Almanac, 1997)*

Country	Total Medals Awarded
United States	101
Germany	65
Russia	63
China	50
Australia	41
France	37
Italy	35
South Korea	27
Cuba	25
Ukraine	23

Practice

5.6

Name _____

In Exercises 1–3, use the bar graph. It shows the top five world's highest dams and their structural height in feet. *(Source: The Information Please Almanac, 1997)*

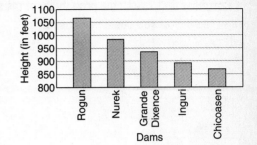

1. By looking at the bars, compare the height of Rogun to the height of Chicoasen.

2. Use the scale to determine the answer to Exercise 1.

3. Explain why the graph is misleading. Then create a bar graph that is not misleading.

4. The line graphs show the winning times for men and for women in the Boston Marathon from 1987–1996. Which graph is misleading? Explain your reasoning. *(Source: The Universal Almanac, 1997)*

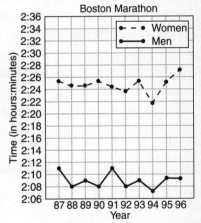

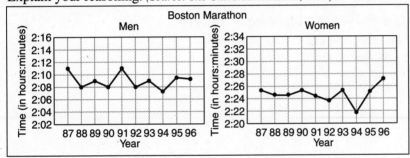

In Exercises 5 and 6, use the bar graphs. They show the amount of education the population of the United States 25 years old and older have reached for the years 1940–1995. Note: Data for 1960 actually 1959, and for 1990 actually 1991. *(Source: The Universal Almanac, 1997)*

5. Explain why the bar graphs are misleading.

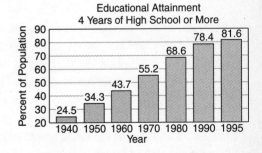

6. Create one bar graph combining both graphs. Be sure that your bar graph is not misleading. Would a line graph also be appropriate for the data? Explain.

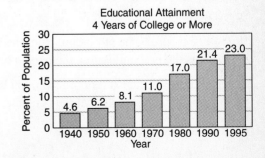

In Exercises 1–3, match the probability of the spinner landing on a shaded area with the spinner you could have used.

a.

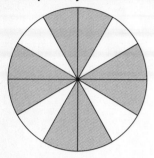

b.

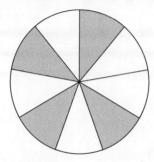

c.

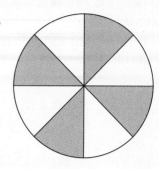

1. 0.5

2. 0.67

3. 0.44

In Exercises 4–6, you are randomly choosing a word from the Preamble of the Constitution of the United States of America which was written in 1787 and ratified in 1789. "We, the people of the United States, in order to form a more perfect union, establish justice, insure domestic tranquility, provide for the common defense, promote the general welfare, and secure the blessing of liberty to ourselves and our posterity, do ordain and establish this Constitution for the United States of America." Find the probabilities of each of the following.

4. The word has three syllables or more.

5. The word has three letters or less.

6. The word contains the letter "e."

7. In a certain town 215 boys and 265 girls were born last year. What is the probability that on a given day when there was only one child born it was a girl?

8. The mail is delivered each day between 1 P.M. and 3:30 P.M. Today is your birthday and you are expecting a package in the mail from your aunt. While waiting for the delivery at the door, the phone rings. You are away from the door for 15 minutes. What is the probability that you missed the delivery?

In Exercises 9 and 10, use the circle graph. It shows the number of people in the United States in 1996 with each blood type.
(Source: America's Blood Centers)

9. A person is selected at random from the United States population. What is the probability that the person has blood type B?

10. A person is selected at random from the United States population. What is the probability that the person does not have blood type B?

United States Blood Types

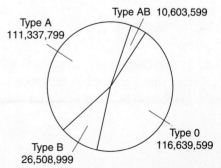

Type A
111,337,799

Type AB 10,603,599

Type O
116,639,599

Type B
26,508,999

In Exercises 1–4, decide whether the quotient is a ratio. Explain your reasoning.

1. $\dfrac{12 \text{ feet}}{8 \text{ feet}}$

2. $\dfrac{7 \text{ miles}}{25 \text{ km}}$

3. $\dfrac{4 \text{ hours}}{90 \text{ minutes}}$

4. $\dfrac{3 \text{ days}}{30 \text{ days}}$

In Exercises 5–8, rewrite the quotient as a ratio.

5. $\dfrac{30 \text{ inches}}{8 \text{ feet}}$

6. $\dfrac{2 \text{ pounds}}{18 \text{ ounces}}$

7. $\dfrac{2 \text{ days}}{15 \text{ hours}}$

8. $\dfrac{12 \text{ pints}}{4 \text{ gallons}}$

In Exercises 9–11, write the ratio of the perimeter of the shaded region to the perimeter of the entire region.

9.
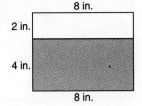

10.
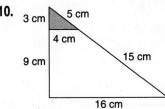

11.
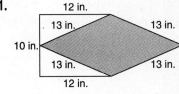

12. Suppose you do homework at night for 90 minutes and are in school each day for eight hours. Find the ratio for the number of minutes that you do homework to the number of minutes that you are in school.

13. You are mixing lemonade to sell on a hot summer day. The recipe requires 300 mL of lemon juice and 2 liters of water. Find the ratio of lemon juice to water.

In Exercises 1–4, simplify the quotient. Is it a rate or a ratio?

1. $\dfrac{1500 \text{ pounds}}{2 \text{ tons}}$

2. $\dfrac{32 \text{ cats}}{18 \text{ cats}}$

3. $\dfrac{90 \text{ feet}}{30 \text{ seconds}}$

4. $\dfrac{24 \text{ points}}{2 \text{ games}}$

In Exercises 5–8, find the unit rate.

5. You run 3 miles in 45 minutes.

6. For mowing 6 lawns, you get paid $34.50.

7. A typist earns $105 for typing 10 pages.

8. A computer does 150,000 calculations in 30 seconds.

In Exercises 9–11, which is a better buy? Explain your answer.

9. **a.** A 20-ounce can of pineapple for $0.90
   b. A 24-ounce can of pineapple for $1.05

10. **a.** A 25-pound crate of oranges for $16
    b. A 20-pound crate of oranges for $13.50

11. **a.** A $27\frac{1}{2}$-ounce jar of spaghetti sauce for $1.89
    b. A 32-ounce jar of spaghetti sauce for $2.05

12. In 1995, there was a total of 11,788 kidney transplants performed in the United States. Find the rate of kidney transplants performed per day in 1995. *(Source: Universal Almanac, 1997)*

13. In 1990, the population of the United States was 248,709,873 people. Also in 1990, there were 143,453,000 passenger cars in the United States. Find the people to car ratio in 1990. *(Source: Universal Almanac, 1997)*

6.3

Name _____

In Exercises 1–3, decide whether the statement is true.

1. $\frac{3}{5} \overset{?}{=} \frac{15}{25}$

2. $\frac{18}{36} \overset{?}{=} \frac{2}{1}$

3. $\frac{24}{36} \overset{?}{=} \frac{16}{24}$

In Exercises 4–7, write the description as a proportion. Then solve the proportion.

4. e is to 8 as 4 is to 16.

5. y is to 20 as 18 is to 72.

6. 75 is to 15 as w is to 5.

7. 80 is to 5 as t is to 3.

In Exercises 8–13, solve the proportion.

8. $\dfrac{3}{5} = \dfrac{y}{20}$

9. $\dfrac{x}{9} = \dfrac{28}{18}$

10. $\dfrac{t}{4} = \dfrac{25}{2}$

11. $\dfrac{k}{40} = \dfrac{12}{48}$

12. $\dfrac{7}{28} = \dfrac{q}{8}$

13. $\dfrac{36}{4} = \dfrac{z}{9}$

14. A car uses 20 gallons of gasoline for a trip of 360 miles. How many gallons of gasoline would be used on a trip of 468 miles?

15. A pump can fill a 750 gallon tank in 90 minutes. How many hours will it take the same pump to fill a 1000 gallon tank?

In Exercises 1–6, use cross products to decide whether the proportion is true.

1. $\dfrac{5}{105} \overset{?}{=} \dfrac{25}{525}$

2. $\dfrac{4}{48} \overset{?}{=} \dfrac{15}{180}$

3. $\dfrac{39}{58.5} \overset{?}{=} \dfrac{16}{24}$

4. $\dfrac{12}{144} \overset{?}{=} \dfrac{16}{256}$

5. $\dfrac{18.5}{37} \overset{?}{=} \dfrac{40.2}{201}$

6. $\dfrac{5.4}{43.2} \overset{?}{=} \dfrac{25}{200}$

In Exercises 7–14, use cross products to solve the proportion. Then check the solution.

7. $\dfrac{3}{8} = \dfrac{k}{48}$

8. $\dfrac{10}{16} = \dfrac{t}{20}$

9. $\dfrac{28}{m} = \dfrac{8}{50}$

10. $\dfrac{2.5}{8} = \dfrac{15}{r}$

11. $\dfrac{25}{16} = \dfrac{q}{40}$

12. $\dfrac{3.8}{b} = \dfrac{17}{51}$

13. $\dfrac{95}{110} = \dfrac{d}{11}$

14. $\dfrac{w}{336} = \dfrac{1}{42}$

In Exercises 15 and 16, show that the polygons have the same width-to-length or base-to-height ratios.

15.

24 in.

8 in.

12 in.

36 in.

16.

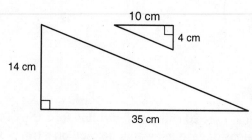

10 cm

4 cm

14 cm

35 cm

In Exercises 17–20, use a calculator to solve the proportion. Round your result to the nearest hundredth.

17. $\dfrac{4}{7} = \dfrac{w}{12}$

18. $\dfrac{11}{18} = \dfrac{15}{f}$

19. $\dfrac{18}{j} = \dfrac{24}{19}$

20. $\dfrac{a}{14} = \dfrac{95}{84}$

In Exercises 1 and 2, decide which of the equations you could *not* use to solve the problem. Then solve the problem.

1. Three cups of flour are required to make 2 dozen cookies. How many cups of flour are required to make 5 dozen cookies?

   a. $\dfrac{3 \text{ cups}}{2 \text{ dozen cookies}} = \dfrac{x \text{ cups}}{5 \text{ dozen cookies}}$

   b. $\dfrac{3 \text{ cups}}{x \text{ cups}} = \dfrac{2 \text{ dozen cookies}}{5 \text{ dozen cookies}}$

   c. $\dfrac{2 \text{ dozen cookies}}{x \text{ cups}} = \dfrac{5 \text{ dozen cookies}}{3 \text{ cups}}$

2. On a map 1 inch represents 25 miles. You measure the distance between two cities on a map and find the distance to be $5\frac{1}{2}$ inches. Find the number of miles between the cities.

   a. $\dfrac{1 \text{ inch}}{5\frac{1}{2} \text{ inches}} = \dfrac{25 \text{ miles}}{x \text{ miles}}$

   b. $\dfrac{1 \text{ inch}}{x \text{ miles}} = \dfrac{5\frac{1}{2} \text{ miles}}{25 \text{ miles}}$

   c. $\dfrac{25 \text{ miles}}{1 \text{ inch}} = \dfrac{x \text{ miles}}{5\frac{1}{2} \text{ inches}}$

In Exercises 3–6, write a proportion. Then solve the problem.

3. If 24 pounds of fertilizer will cover 1750 square feet, how many pounds of fertilizer will be needed to cover 6562.5 square feet?

4. A chemistry experiment requires a saltwater solution. Your instructor wants you to mix the solution. The correct ratio of salt to water is 2 grams of salt to 5 liters of water. You need one liter for each of the 28 students in class. How many grams of salt will this require?

5. In a public opinion poll, 9 out of every 16 people indicated that they would vote for a particular candidate in an upcoming election. Assuming this poll is accurate, how many votes can the candidate expect to receive from 30,000 votes cast?

6. You are filling a small above-ground pool. It has taken the pump 36 minutes to pump 750 gallons of water. If the pool requires 1000 gallons, how much longer will it take to fill the pool?

In Exercises 1 and 2, show that the two polygons are similar.

1.

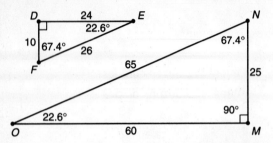

2.

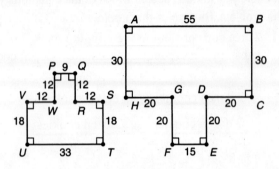

In Exercises 3–6, the figures are similar. Find the missing measures.

3.

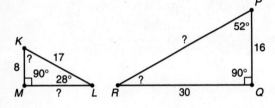

4.

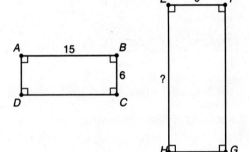

5.

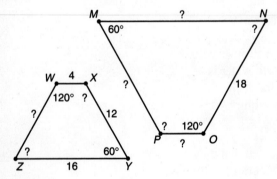

6.

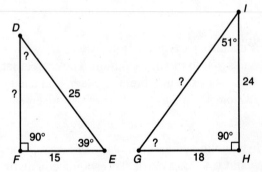

7. You are standing 16 feet from the base of the flag pole. Both your shadow and the pole's shadow extend to the same point 4 feet from you. You are 5 feet tall. Find the height of the flag pole.

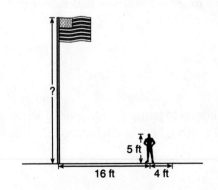

In Exercises 1–4, the scale of a map is 2 cm to 25 miles. You are given the distance on the map. Find the actual distance.

1. 12 cm

2. 10 cm

3. 1.5 cm

4. 34.4 cm

In Exercises 5 and 6, find the perimeter of the actual object using the scale factor shown on the blueprint.

5.

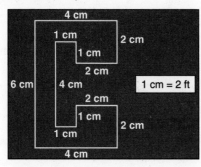

6.

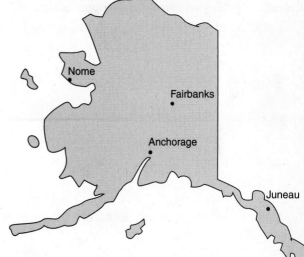

In Exercises 7–11, use the map of Alaska. The scale factor is 2 cm to 250 miles. Use a centimeter ruler to find the distances between the cities.

7. Nome and Fairbanks

8. Juneau and Anchorage

9. Fairbanks and Juneau

10. Anchorage and Fairbanks

11. Nome and Juneau

12. You are designing a dog house for the Labrador puppy that you received for your birthday. The scale factor for your design is 0.5 inch to 1 foot. Label the actual dimensions of the dog house. What is the total surface to be painted on the house (both ends, sides and roof)?

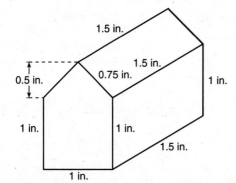

Name _____

In Exercises 1–4, write the percent as (a) a decimal and (b) a fraction in simplest form.

1. 10%   **2.** 30%   **3.** 75%   **4.** 95%

In Exercises 5–8, write the decimal as a fraction with a denominator of 100, then as a percent.

5. 0.84   **6.** 0.07   **7.** 0.015   **8.** 0.6

In Exercises 9–12, write the fraction as a percent.

9. $\frac{7}{25}$ **10.** $\frac{2}{5}$ **11.** $\frac{5}{8}$ **12.** $\frac{17}{20}$

In Exercises 13–15, what percent of the figure is shaded?

13. 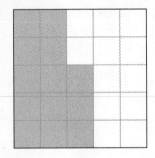   **14.** 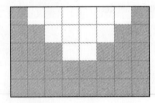   **15.**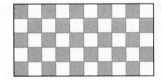

In Exercises 16 and 17, which number doesn't belong in the list? Explain.

16. $0.76, \frac{19}{25}, 76\%, \frac{38}{50}, \frac{38}{100}$ **17.** $\frac{4}{15}, 26.7\%, \frac{26.7}{100}, \frac{28}{95}, \frac{8}{30}$

18. Three hundred people were surveyed and reported that they rearrange their furniture in their homes for several different reasons. The results are shown in the graph. Write the results as percents.

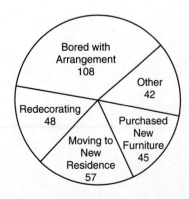

In Exercises 1–3, write a percent to represent the shaded area. Then find the number represented by the percent.

1. 100 squares = 250 marbles

2. 100 squares = 25 quarters

3. 100 squares = 1000 pencils

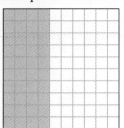 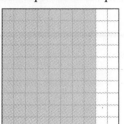 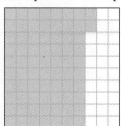

In Exercises 4–6, use a unit square model to find the number.

4. 70% of 150 miles

5. 40% of 20 students

6. 5% of $500

In Exercises 7–14, write each percent as a decimal. Then find the percent.

7. 15% of 120

8. 78% of 350

9. 12% of 250

10. 98% of 500

11. 2% of 500

12. 64% of 50

13. 84% of 425

14. 55% of 20

In Exercises 15 and 16, use the given information to estimate the percent.

15. Estimate 65% of 130. Given 60% of 130 = 78 and 70% of 130 = 91.

16. Estimate 45% of 20. Given 40% of 20 = 8 and 50% of 20 = 10.

17. During a given winter, there was 120 inches of snow. Of that total 35% fell in January. How many inches of snow fell in January?

18. Because of slumping sales, a small company laid off 45% of its 180 employees. How many employees were laid off?

In Exercises 1–4, write the percent as (a) a decimal and (b) a fraction in simplest form.

1. 150% **2.** $\frac{1}{5}\%$ **3.** $\frac{7}{8}\%$ **4.** 325%

In Exercises 5–12, write the fraction or decimal as a percent.

5. 1.25 **6.** $\frac{15}{2}$ **7.** $\frac{2}{500}$ **8.** 0.0025

9. $\frac{91}{50}$ **10.** 5.35 **11.** 0.0005 **12.** $\frac{7}{1250}$

In Exercises 13–15, use mental math to estimate the number.

13. 150% of $\$200$ **14.** 180% of 500 coins   **15.** $\frac{1}{2}\%$ of 4000 miles

In Exercises 16–21, complete the statement using <, >, or =.

16. 275% $\boxed{?}$ $\frac{11}{4}$ **17.** 0.00625 $\boxed{?}$ 62.5% **18.** $\frac{1}{5}\%$ $\boxed{?}$ 0.2

19. 4.50 $\boxed{?}$ $\frac{9}{2}$ **20.** $\frac{1}{8}\%$ $\boxed{?}$ 0.000125 **21.** $\frac{17}{25}\%$ $\boxed{?}$ 0.068

22. A company that manufactures light bulbs states that less than $\frac{2}{5}\%$ of all light bulbs manufactured per day are defective. If the company produced 15,000 light bulbs on a given day how many light bulbs could be expected to be defective?

23. Because of a membership drive for a community center, the current membership is 125% of what is was a year ago. The membership last year was 7400 members. How many members does the community center have this year?

In Exercises 1–4, use a percent equation to solve the problem.

1. The seating capacity of a university football stadium was increased by 35%. The old capacity was 68,000. What is the new seating capacity?

2. The enrollment of a small local college is 3,500. Approximately 32% of the enrollment are freshman. About how many freshman are enrolled?

3. You have decided to trade in your mountain bike for a new one. The bike shop stated that they can give you 42% of the price of the old bike or $226.80 toward the new one. What was the price of your old bike?

4. The news media reported that 6,435 votes were cast in the last election and that this represented 65% of the eligible voters of that district. How many eligible voters are in the district?

In Exercises 5–12, solve the percent problem.

5. What is 35% of 80?

6. What is 82% of 500?

7. What percent of 850 is 238?

8. 51 is what percent of 340?

9. 14% of what number is 84?

10. 299 is 65% of what number?

11. $\frac{1}{2}$% of what number is 5?

12. 18 is 225% of what number?

In Exercises 13–15, solve the percent problem.

13. You and your family are traveling to the mountains for a week of vacation. On the first day of driving, your family has driven 385 miles. If the total trip is 550 miles, what percent of the driving have you completed?

14. A popular soft drink has a new advertisement campaign stating that for the same price you get 33 1/3% more. The bottles used to contain 12 ounces, so now they will contain how much?

15. Rich Bucks is trying to save money to buy a used car. He wants to save 18% of his monthly earnings or $585. How much does Rich earn per month?

In Exercises 1–3, use the circle graph at the right. It shows the results of a survey in which 200 middle school students were asked to name their favorite summer time activity.

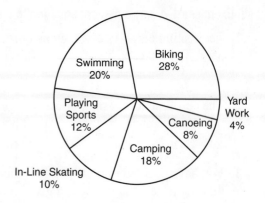

1. How many students chose biking?

2. How many more students chose swimming than camping?

3. How many times as many students chose playing sports as chose yard work?

In Exercises 4 and 5, make a circle graph of the data.

4. The percents of sales of recorded music in the United States in 1995 classified by type are: rock (33.5%), country (16.7%), popular (10.1%), urban contemporary (11.3%), Rap (6.7%), classical (2.9%), jazz (3.0%), gospel (3.1%), other (12.7%). *(Source: Universal Almanac, 1997)*

5. The percents of energy consumption in the United States in 1994 classified by source of fuel are: petroleum products (39.2%), natural gas (23.9%), coal (22.1%), nuclear power (7.7%), hydro-electric (3.5%), other (3.6%). *(Source: Universal Almanac, 1997)*

In Exercises 6–8, use the table at the right. It shows both the percents of land coverage and population of all seven continents of the world as of 1992. *(Source: Universal Almanac, 1997)*

Continent	Land Coverage	Population
Africa	20.4%	12.1%
Antarctica	8.9%	0%
Asia	30.0%	61.2%
Australia	5.2%	0.3%
Europe	7.1%	12.6%
North America	16.3%	8.1%
South America	12.0%	5.5%

6. Make circle graphs of both land coverage by continent and population by continent.

7. The total land coverage of the world is 57,308,757 square miles. Find the area of the continent with the largest land coverage.

8. The world population was 5,420,391,000 in 1992. Determine the approximate population of North America in 1992.

In Exercises 1–4, you deposit $4000 in a savings account that pays 3% annual interest. Find the simple interest you earn for the given amount of time.

1. 3 months   **2.** 6 months   **3.** 8 months   **4.** 12 months

In Exercises 5–8, you borrow $6000 from a bank. Find the amount of simple interest you will pay after 24 months with the given interest rate.

5. 8%   **6.** 10%   **7.** 12%   **8.** 16%

In Exercises 9–11, find the interest earned for depositing the given principal in an account with the given interest rate for the listed amount of time. Then find the account balance.

9. $P = \$500$
$r = 6\%$
$t = 8$ months

10. $P = \$1500$
$r = 4\%$
$t = 18$ months

11. $P = \$6500$
$r = 6.5\%$
$t = 30$ months

In Exercises 12–14, find the interest you will pay for borrowing the given principal under the given conditions. Then find the total you must pay back.

12. $P = \$11,500$
$r = 12\%$
$t = 10$ months

13. $P = \$4500$
$r = 8.5\%$
$t = 4$ months

14. $P = \$16,000$
$r = 10\%$
$t = 24$ months

15. You deposit $5000 in a savings account. Use the Guess, Check and Revise method to determine what interest rate you would have to get to earn $325 in interest for 1 year.

16. You deposit $6000 in a savings account. Use the Guess, Check and Revise method to determine how long it would take to earn $810 while earning 9% simple interest.

In Exercises 1–8, find the percent increase or decrease.

1. Before: 50   After: 75

2. Before: 36   After: 63

3. Before: 120 After: 78

4. Before: 160 After: 136

5. Before: 240 After: 396

6. Before: 84   After: 105

7. Before: 95   After: 133

8. Before: 480 After: 24

9. The volume of first class mail handled by the U.S. Postal service in 1994 was 94,376 million pieces of mail. In 1995, the total was 96,296 million pieces of mail. Find the percent increase or decrease in volume of first class mail handled. *(Source: Universal Almanac, 1997)*

In Exercises 10–13, use the table at the right. It shows the 1980 and 1990 populations (in thousands) for different states. Find the percent increase or decrease. *(Source: Universal Almanac, 1997)*

State	1980	1990
Alaska	401.9	550.0
Nevada	800.5	1201.8
Iowa	2913.8	2776.8
West Virginia	1949.6	1793.5

10. Alaska

11. Nevada

12. Iowa

13. West Virginia

In Exercises 14 and 15, use the table at the right. It shows the number of drive-in and indoor theaters in 1980, 1990, and 1995.
(Source: Universal Almanac, 1997)

Year	Drive-In	Indoor
1980	3561	14,029
1990	915	22,774
1995	847	26,958

14. Find the percent increase or decrease for drive-in theaters from 1980 to 1995.

15. Find the percent increase or decrease for indoor theaters from 1980 to 1995.

Practice 8.1

Name _____

In Exercises 1–4, use the figure at the right to write the measure of each angle. The lines *a* and *b* are parallel.

1. ∠1   **2.** ∠3   **3.** ∠5   **4.** ∠6

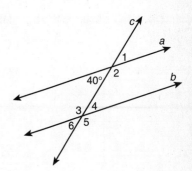

In Exercises 5–7, complete the statement using *vertical, parallel, intersecting* or *corresponding*.

5. If two parallel lines are intersected by a third line, then the _____ angles are congruent.

6. Intersecting lines form congruent _____ angles.

7. Two lines that never meet are called _____ lines.

8. Two lines that are not parallel are called _____ lines.

In Exercises 9–11, write the angles that are congruent to ∠2.

9.
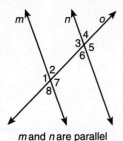
m and *n* are parallel

10.
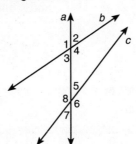

11.
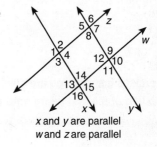
x and *y* are parallel
w and *z* are parallel

In Exercises 12–14, find the measures of the angles. Explain how you solved the problem.

12.
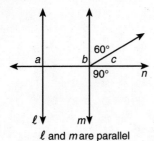
ℓ and *m* are parallel

13.
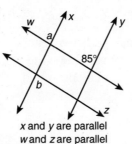
x and *y* are parallel
w and *z* are parallel

14.
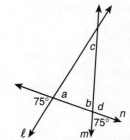

In Exercises 15 and 16, use the diagram at the right. It shows a road map for a portion of a large city interstate highway system.

15. Which pairs of interstate routes appear parallel?

16. Find the measures of angles labeled a, b, c, d, and e.

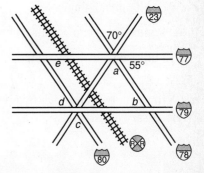

In Exercises 1–3, describe the translation of the unshaded figure to the shaded figure.

1.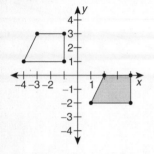

2.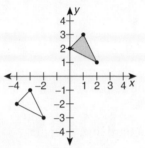

3.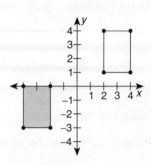

In Exercises 4 and 5, you are given the coordinates of a figure. Write the coordinates of the translated figure. Then check your result by graphing both figures.

4. $A(2, 3)$, $B(4, -1)$, $C(-4, 0)$; 5 units down and 1 unit left

5. $J(-2, 4)$, $K(2, 4)$, $L(4, 7)$, $M(-4, 7)$; 2 units right and 4 units down

In Exercises 6 and 7, you are given the coordinates of two figures. Describe the translation of the first figure onto the second figure.

6. $W(3, -4)$, $X(-2, 1)$, $Y(-2, 4)$, $Z(3, 1)$ onto $A(-1, -2)$, $B(-6, 3)$, $C(-6, 6)$, $D(-1, 3)$

7. $J(-7, 5)$, $K(1, 3)$, $L(-2, 1)$ onto $M(-5, 4)$, $N(3, 2)$, $O(0, 0)$

8. Find the name of Carl's dog. The dog's name has five letters. To find the dog's name, start at (1, 1) on the grid and write down the coordinates and letter. Use the translations to find the position of the other letters.

  1. Start at (1, 1).

  2. 3 units down and 2 units right

  3. 1 unit up and 4 units left

  4. 3 units down and 3 units right

  5. 5 units up and 4 units left

9. Write your own message by giving a starting point and the necessary translations.

In Exercises 1–3, find the circumference of the circle. Use 3.14 for π.

1.

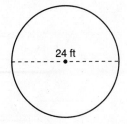

24 ft

2.

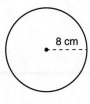

8 cm

3.

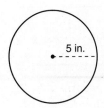

5 in.

In Exercises 4–6, match the object with its circumference.

a. 1.25 feet   **b.** 0.1 foot   **c.** 2.2 feet

4. An aspirin   **5.** A car headlight   **6.** A compact disc

In Exercises 7–9, find the dimension labeled x.

7. Circumference = 94.2 in.

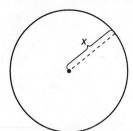

8. Circumference = 59.66 yds

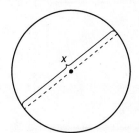

9. Circumference = 75.4 cm

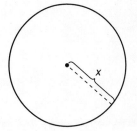

In Exercises 10–13, find the circumference of the figure. Use 3.14 for π.

10.

Frisbee

$r = 6.1$ in.

11.

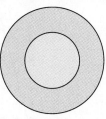

$d = 2.2$ in.

12.

DO NOT ENTER

$d = 2.8$ ft

13.

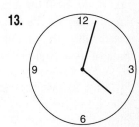

$d = 14.2$ in.

Washington, D.C. **In Exercise 14, use the map at the right.**

14. The road around Washington, D.C., is called the *Beltway*. Estimate the length of a trip on the Beltway around the entire city.

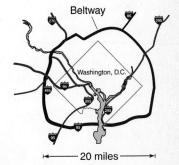

Beltway

Washington, D.C.

← 20 miles →

In Exercises 1–3, find the area of the parallelogram.

1.
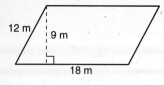
12 m   9 m   18 m

2.
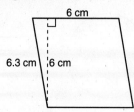
6 cm   6.3 cm   6 cm

3.
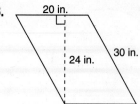
20 in.   24 in.   30 in.

In Exercises 4–6, on dot paper draw two different parallelograms that have the given area.

4. 8 square units   **5.** 24 square units   **6.** 40 square units

In Exercises 7–9, find the missing measure of each parallelogram.

7. $A = 360$ sq in.
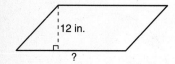
12 in.   ?

8. $A = 180$ sq cm
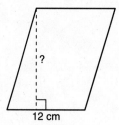
?   12 cm

9. $A = 605$ sq yd
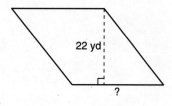
22 yd   ?

10. Divide the parallelogram into two triangles and a rectangle. Find the area of each part. Then add the three areas to obtain the area of the parallelogram. Compare the result with that obtained using the formula for the area of a parallelogram.

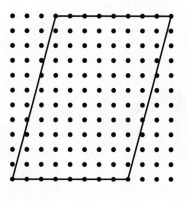

In Exercises 11 and 12, use the map to estimate the area of the state.

11.

Missouri
132 miles

12.
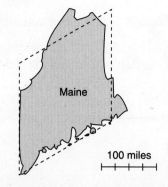
Maine
100 miles

In Exercises 1–3, decide whether the figure is a trapezoid. If it is, find its height and area.

1.

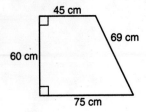

45 cm
69 cm
60 cm
75 cm

2.

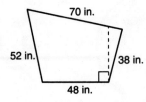

70 in.
52 in.
38 in.
48 in.

3.

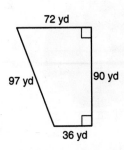

72 yd
97 yd
90 yd
36 yd

In Exercises 4–7, find the area of the trapezoid.

4. $b_1 = 4$ cm, $b_2 = 6$ cm, $h = 12$ cm

5. $b_1 = 5.5$ in., $b_2 = 10.25$ in., $h = 18$ in.

6. $b_1 = 10$ cm, $b_2 = 16$ cm, $h = 28$ cm

7. $b_1 = 200$ yd, $b_2 = 350$ yd, $h = 125$ yd

In Exercises 8–10, on each trapezoid find the dimension labeled x.

8.

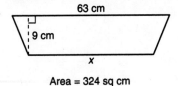

63 cm
9 cm
x
Area = 324 sq cm

9.

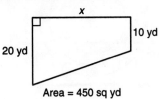

x
10 yd
20 yd
Area = 450 sq yd

10.

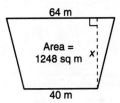

64 m
Area = 1248 sq m
x
40 m

In Exercises 11–13, find the area of the region.

11.

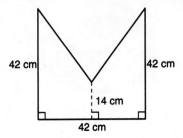

42 cm
42 cm
14 cm
42 cm

12.

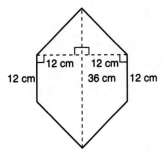

12 cm   12 cm
12 cm
36 cm
12 cm

13.

16 in.   8 in.   8 in.   16 in.
4 in.
4 in.

14. The garage roof shown in the figure is made from two trapezoids and two triangles. Find the area of the entire roof.

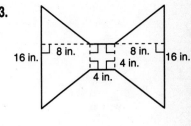

15 ft
30 ft
15 ft
30 ft
60 ft

In Exercises 1–4, find the area of the object. Use π = 3.14. Round to two decimal places.

1.

$r = 6.1$ in.

2.

$d = 2.2$ in.

3.

$d = 2.8$ ft

4.

$r = 14.2$ in.

In Exercises 5-8, find the area and circumference of a circle with the given measurement.

5. Radius = 4 ft

6. Diameter = 36 cm

7. Diameter = 18 yd

8. Radius = 42 km

In Exercises 9–11, find the area of the shaded region.

9.

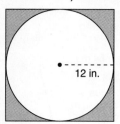

12 in.

10.

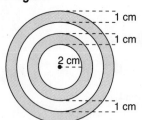

1 cm
1 cm
2 cm
1 cm

11.

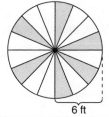

6 ft

In Exercises 12–14, find the radius and area of the object. Use π = 3.14. Round your result to one decimal place.

12.

$C = 96.1$ in.

13.

$C = 57.8$ cm

14.

$C = 37.7$ cm

15. A semicircular arch for a tunnel under a river has a diameter of 100 feet. Determine the area of the cross section under the arch.

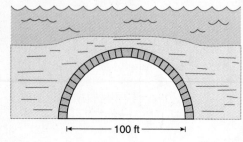

100 ft

16. A stained glass window has a circumference of 28.26 feet. Find the radius and the area of the window.

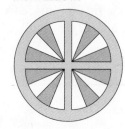

In Exercises 1–8, use a calculator to find the square root of the number. Round your result to two decimal places.

1. $\sqrt{36}$ **2.** $\sqrt{144}$ **3.** $\sqrt{529}$ **4.** $\sqrt{70.56}$

5. $\sqrt{24.01}$ **6.** $\sqrt{14}$ **7.** $\sqrt{80}$ **8.** $\sqrt{56.5}$

In Exercises 9–11, find the value of s. Explain your method.

9. A = 102.01 sq ft

s

10. A = 138.24 sq cm

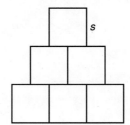

s

11. A = 169.28 sq in.

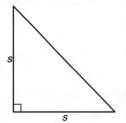

s

s

In Exercises 12–19, use mental math to estimate the square root. Then use a calculator to check your estimate.

12. $\sqrt{8}$ **13.** $\sqrt{20}$ **14.** $\sqrt{85}$ **15.** $\sqrt{170}$

16. $\sqrt{48}$ **17.** $\sqrt{68}$ **18.** $\sqrt{390}$ **19.** $\sqrt{630}$

20. A square room has 729 square feet of floor space. An area carpet covers all of the floor space except for a one-foot border all around the room. How many square feet of carpeting is there?

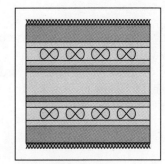

In Exercises 1–3, decide whether the triangle is right, acute or obtuse. If it is a
right triangle, name the hypotenuse.

1.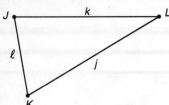

2.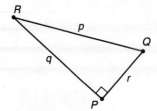

3.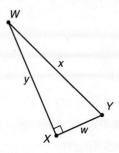

In Exercises 4–6, find the length of the hypotenuse.

4.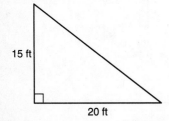

5.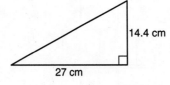

6.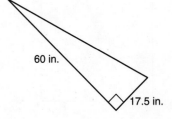

In Exercises 7–9, you are given the lengths of the legs of a right triangle. Find
the length of the hypotenuse. Round your result to the nearest hundredth.

7. $a = 20, b = 30$

8. $a = 45, b = 85$

9. $a = 28, b = 120$

In Exercises 10–12, find the length of the missing side of the right triangle.

10.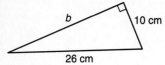

11.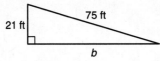

12.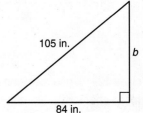

13. A plane flies in a straight line from Osceola, 100 miles
east and 150 miles north to Jacksonville. How far did the
plane fly?

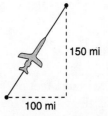

14. During a football game, a quarterback throws a pass from
the 15-yard line, 10 yards from the sideline. The pass is
caught on the 40-yard line, 45 yards from the same
sideline. How many yards did the ball actually travel in
the air?

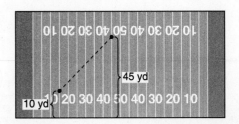

Practice

9.1

In Exercises 1–4, decide whether the figure is a polyhedron. If it is, name the polyhedron.

1.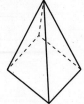

2.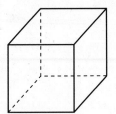

3.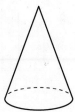

4.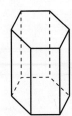

In Exercises 5–10, draw the solid formed from the net. Name the type of figure that is formed.

5.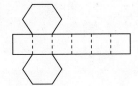

6.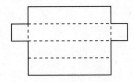

7.

8.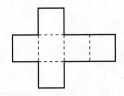

9.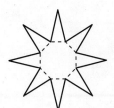

10.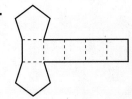

11. Use the figure that represents a barn.

    a. Name the type of figure.

    b. How many faces does the barn have?

    c. How many edges does the barn have?

    d. How many vertices does the barn have?

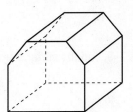

12. Use the figure that represents a piece of cake.

    a. Name the type of figure.

    b. How many faces does the piece of cake have?

    c. How many edges does the piece of cake have?

    d. How many vertices does the piece of cake have?

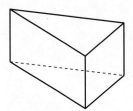

13. Use the figure that represents a 30-story beach front condominium.

    a. Name the type of figure.

    b. How many faces does the condominium have?

    c. How many edges does the condominium have?

    d. How many vertices does the condominium have?

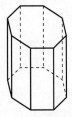

In Exercises 1–3, match the net with the prism. What is the surface area of the prism?

a.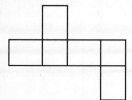

b.

c.

1.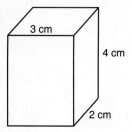
3 cm
4 cm
2 cm

2.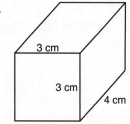
3 cm
3 cm
4 cm

3.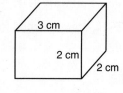
3 cm
2 cm
2 cm

In Exercises 4–6, find the surface area of the prism.

4.
1.5 in.
DRINK BOX
4.25 in.
2.5 in.

5.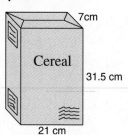
7cm
Cereal
31.5 cm
21 cm

6.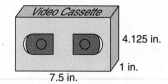
Video Cassette
4.125 in.
1 in.
7.5 in.

In Exercises 7–9, find the surface area of the solid.

7.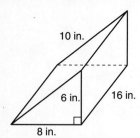
10 in.
6 in. 16 in.
8 in.

8.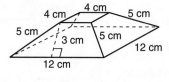
4 cm 4 cm 5 cm
5 cm 3 cm 5 cm
12 cm 12 cm

9.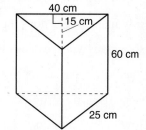
40 cm
15 cm
60 cm
25 cm

In Exercises 10 and 11, use the blocks at the right. Each block is 3 inches by 3 inches by 3 inches.

10. Find the surface area of one cube.

11. Imagine that the blocks are placed side by side to spell "APE." Find the surface area of the new solid.

In Exercises 1–4, decide whether the net can be folded to form a cylinder.

1.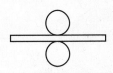

2.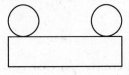

3.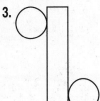

4.

In Exercises 5–7, find the surface area of the cylinder.

5.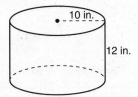
10 in.
12 in.

6.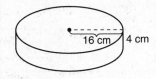
16 cm / 4 cm

7.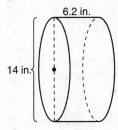
6.2 in.
14 in.

In Exercises 8–11, match the figure with its dimensions. Then find the surface area of the figure.

a. $h = 4.5$ in., $r = 1.5$ in.

b. $h = 7.8$ in., $r = 3.4$ in.

c. $h = 21.2$ cm, $r = 3.8$ cm

d. $h = 78$ mm, $r = 7$ mm

8.
AA Battery

9.
Vegetable Soup

10.
1 Gal. Paint

11.
Tennis Balls

12. Each of the containers holds the same amount of liquid. Just by looking at the containers, which do you think has the least surface area? Check your guess by actually finding the surface area of each container.

a.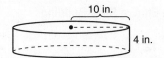
10 in.
4 in.

b.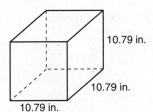
10.79 in.
10.79 in.
10.79 in.

c.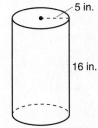
5 in.
16 in.

In Exercises 1–3, match the blueprint with the object.

a.

b.

c.

1.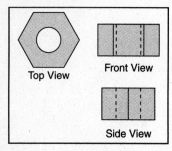

Top View   Front View

Side View

2.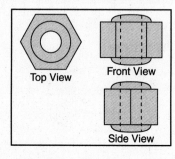

Top View   Front View

Side View

3.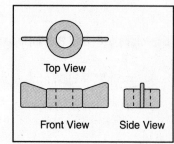

Top View

Front View   Side View

In Exercises 4–6, draw a top view, a front view, and a side view of the object.

4.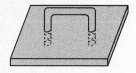

5.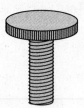

6.

In Exercises 7–9, use the view to name the solid.

7.

Top

Front   Side

8.

Top

Front   Side

9.

Top

Front   Side

In Exercises 10–12, match the top view with the building.

a. The Pentagon

b. The Houston Astrodome

c. The Empire State Building

10.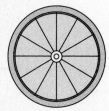

11.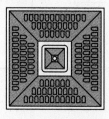

12.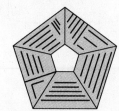

<table>
<tr><td>

Practice
</td><td>

9.5
</td><td>

Name _____
</td></tr>
</table>

In Exercises 1–3, find the volume of the object.

1.

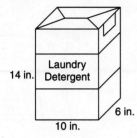

14 in. | Laundry Detergent
6 in.
10 in.

2.

DRINK BOX

10 cm

5 cm | 7 cm

3.

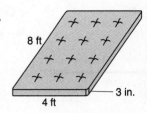

8 ft

3 in.

4 ft

In Exercises 4–7, sketch each rectangular prism. Then find its volume.

4. 8 ft by 6 ft by 4 ft

5. 15.3 cm by 12.5 cm by 9.2 cm

6. 5.25 m by 6.5 m by 10.4 m

7. $5\frac{1}{3}$ yds by 6 yds by $8\frac{2}{3}$ yds

In Exercises 8–10, find the surface area and the volume of the rectangular prism.

8.

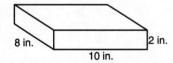

8 in.
10 in.
2 in.

9.

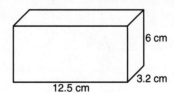

6 cm
12.5 cm
3.2 cm

10.

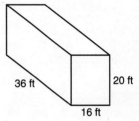

36 ft
16 ft
20 ft

In Exercises 11–13, find the dimension labeled x.

11. Volume = 300 cu cm

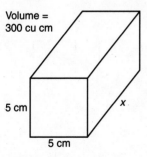

5 cm
5 cm
x

12.

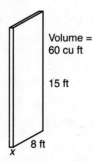

Volume = 60 cu ft

15 ft

x | 8 ft

13. Volume = 1820 cu cm

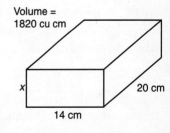

x
14 cm
20 cm

14. A large fish tank in the shape of a rectangular prism is 24 inches high, and has a base that is 18 inches wide and 36 inches long. You are filling the tank with water to a height of 22 inches. If water is being pumped in at a rate of 2 cubic inches per second, how many minutes will it take to reach the proper level?

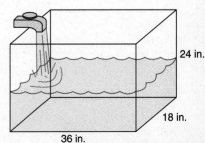

24 in.

36 in.

18 in.

In Exercises 1–4, use a calculator to find the volume of the cylinder.

1.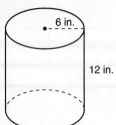
6 in.

12 in.

2.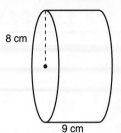
8 cm

9 cm

3.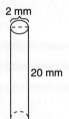
2 mm

20 mm

4.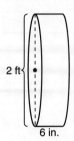
2 ft

6 in.

In Exercises 5–8, use the Guess, Check and Revise method to find the height or the radius of the cylinder.

5.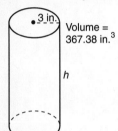
3 in.

Volume = 367.38 in.^{3}

h

6. Volume = 1607.68 cm^3
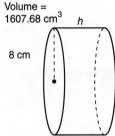
8 cm

h

7.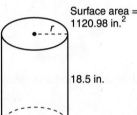
r

18.5 in.

Surface area = 1120.98 in.^{2}

8.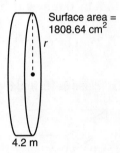
Surface area = 1808.64 cm^2

r

4.2 m

9. Determine the dimensions and the volume of the largest cylinder that can be placed inside a box that has dimensions 14 in. by 7 in. by 2 in. Explain your reasoning. How much extra space is there inside the box?

10. A cylindrical barrel 3 feet high has a base with radius of 18 inches. You are filling the barrel with sand. If the sand weighs 0.86 ounces per cubic inch and the empty barrel weighs 5 pounds, what will the total weight be when the barrel is full?

11. A large cylindrical corn silo on a farm in Nebraska is 24 feet high and has a base with radius of 8 feet. How much corn could the silo contain if it was completely full?

12. You work for a bakery on weekends. One of the specialities of the shop is to bake cakes in the shape of letters of the alphabet. What is the volume of the cake in the shape of the letter "O" if it has given dimensions?

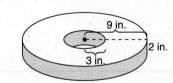
9 in.

3 in.

2 in.

Practice

9.7

Name _____

In Exercises 1 and 2, decide whether the two prisms are similar. If they are similar, find the ratio of the smaller prism to larger prism.

1.

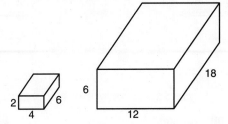

2.

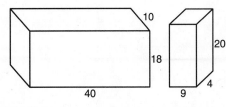

In Exercises 3 and 4, the two rectangular prisms are similar. Find the missing dimensions.

3. **Prism A:** Length = 150 cm
   Width = ?
   Height = 75 cm

   Prism B: Length = ?
   Width = 35 cm
   Height = 15 cm

4. **Prism A:** Length = 24 ft
   Width = 36 ft
   Height = ?

   Prism B: Length = ?
   Width = 24 cm
   Height = 60 cm

In Exercises 5 and 6, the prisms are similar. Find the dimensions labeled x and y.

5.

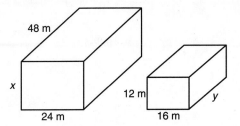

6.

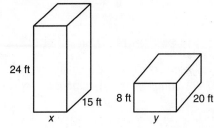

7. You are building a scale model of a log cabin. The scale for your model is 1 inch to 2 feet. The diagram shows the dimensions of the actual cabin. Label the model's dimensions.

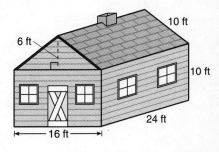

8. You have purchased a scale model of a Jeep. The scale factor is 1 to 24. To keep your model safe you have also bought a plastic container to store the model. If the container has the given dimensions, what would be the actual dimensions in feet of a plastic container to store an actual size Jeep?

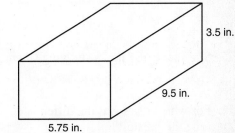

In Exercises 1–4, graph the integer and its absolute value.

1. 5

2. −3

3. 7

4. −10

In Exercises 5–8, write the absolute value expression modeled by the number line.

5.
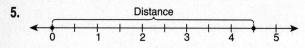

6.
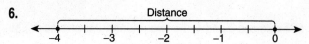

7.
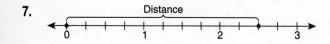

8.
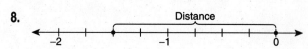

In Exercises 9–16, find the absolute value.

9. $|8|$

10. $|-5|$

11. $|-8|$

12. $|-5.2|$

13. $|8.2|$

14. $|1.6|$

15. $|-0.5|$

16. $|-15|$

In Exercises 17–22, complete the statement using <, >, or =.

17. 15 ☐? $|-12|$

18. $|-4|$ ☐? $|-8|$

19. 7 ☐? $|-7|$

20. 0 ☐? $|-11|$

21. −13 ☐? $|-12|$

22. $|-15|$ ☐? $|-15.5|$

In Exercises 23–26, use the table. It shows a schedule for the amount of time that a college student is going to devote to each of her classes to study for final exams. Decide how much more or less time was actually spent on each course.

Class	Time
Calculus	9 hours
American History	7 hours
Chemistry	8 hours

23. She spent 7.25 hours studying Calculus.

24. She spent 9.75 hours studying American History.

25. She spent 9.25 hours studying Chemistry.

26. For which class was the difference of the scheduled time and actual time the greatest?

In Exercises 1–4, without solving the problem, decide whether the sum is positive, negative or zero. Then find the sum.

1. $-8 + 5$

2. $-15 + (-12)$

3. $(-9) + 9$

4. $-4 + 8$

In Exercises 5–12, find the sum.

5. $-8 + 15$

6. $-15 + (-3)$

7. $15 + (-12)$

8. $10 + (-10)$

9. $-8 + (-12)$

10. $-22 + (-16)$

11. $32 + (-45)$

12. $28 + (-22)$

In Exercises 13–18, solve the equation. Then check the solution.

13. $x - 15 = 18$

14. $y + (-12) = -16$

15. $16 = -20 + f$

16. $-8 + d = 19$

17. $-14 = q + (-2)$

18. $18 + p = -12$

In Exercises 19–21, use a calculator to find the average of the numbers.

19. $-18, 20, -23$

20. $16, -18, 22, -32$

21. $-5, 12, -17, 20, 0$

In Exercises 22–25, find a positive integer and a negative integer that have the indicated sum.

22. 6

23. -5

24. -10

25. 4

26. The table shows the amount of money that a certain stock gained and lost for a week. Find the value of the stock at the end of the week. The stock was worth $14 per share on Monday morning.

Day	Mon	Tues	Wed	Thu	Fri
Value	−$5	+$4	+$3	+$2	−$3

In Exercises 1–8, write each subtraction expression as an equivalent addition expression. Then find the sum.

1. $5 - 16$ **2.** $0 - 15$ **3.** $-5 - 1$ **4.** $-4 - 18$

5. $0 - (-10)$ **6.** $-15 - (-3)$ **7.** $25 - (-12)$ **8.** $-1 - (-1)$

In Exercises 9–16, add or subtract.

9. $5 + (-18)$ **10.** $-15 - (-12)$ **11.** $-12 + (-12)$ **12.** $-13 - 7$

13. $-20 - (-42)$ **14.** $13 - (-12)$ **15.** $-16 + (-18)$ **16.** $16 - (-19)$

In Exercises 17–20, evaluate the expression when $x = 5$ and when $x = -3$.

17. $x - 6$ **18.** $15 - x$ **19.** $-x - 6$ **20.** $-x - (-8)$

In Exercises 21–23, match the expression with the calculator keystrokes. Then evaluate it using a calculator.

a. $15 \boxed{-} 24 \boxed{+/-} \boxed{=}$ **b.** $15 \boxed{-} 24 \boxed{=}$ **c.** $15 \boxed{+/-} \boxed{-} 24 \boxed{=}$

21. $15 - 24$ **22.** $-15 - 24$ **23.** $15 - (-24)$

In Exercises 1–3, complete the table of values.

1. $y = -5 - x$

x	−5	−3	−1	1	3
y					

2. $y = x - 4$

x	8	4	0	−4	−8
y					

3. $y = 5 - x$

x	−4	−2	0	2	4
y					

In Exercises 4–6, write the ordered pairs shown in the table of values. Then plot the points and describe the pattern of the graph.

4.

x	−2	−1	0	1	2
y	−5	−4	−3	−2	−1

5.

x	−2	−1	0	1	2
y	0	−1	−2	−3	−4

6.

x	−2	−1	0	1	2
y	6	5	4	3	2

In Exercises 7–9, make a table of values. Use the x-values of −4, −3, −2, −1, 0, 1, 2, 3 and 4. Then plot the points and describe any patterns.

7. $y = x + 1$

8. $y = -1 + x$

9. $y = -4 - x$

In Exercises 10–12, match the scatter plot with its equation.

a. $y = x - 3$ **b.** $y = x + 2$ **c.** $y = -2 - x$

10.

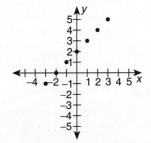

11.

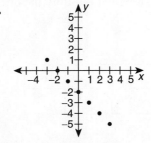

12.

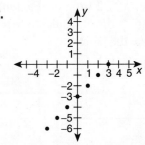

In Exercises 1–6, without solving the problem, decide whether the value is positive, negative, or zero.

1. $-5 - (-5)$

2. $-8 + 9$

3. 2×18

4. $4(-3)$

5. $-4 \times (-6)$

6. $8 \times (-8)$

In Exercises 7–12, find the product.

7. $2 \cdot 18$

8. $(-8)(5)$

9. 2×0

10. $(-5)(-1)(2)$

11. $(2)(-3)(4)$

12. $(11)(-12)(0)$

In Exercises 13–18, use mental math to solve the equation. Check your solution.

13. $w \times 8 = 64$

14. $-5 \times q = -25$

15. $3t = -9$

16. $n \cdot (-6) = 24$

17. $12d = -24$

18. $-27 = s \times (-9)$

In Exercises 19–21, use a calculator to find the product.

19. $15.6 \times (-12.2)$

20. $\frac{2}{3}(-216)$

21. $(-15)(26)(-18.5)$

In Exercises 22–24, evaluate the expression for $x = -4$.

22. $x \cdot (-9)$

23. $\frac{1}{16}x$

24. $(-3) \cdot x \cdot x$

25. To convert from a Fahrenheit temperature F to a Celsius temperature C subtract 32 from the Fahrenheit temperature and multiply the difference by $\frac{5}{9}$. Write an equation to represent this sentence. Then use it to complete the table.

F	5	23	50	68	86	95	104
C							

Practice

10.6

Name _____

In Exercises 1–4, without solving the problem, decide whether the quotient is positive or negative.

1. $-55 \div 11$ **2.** $56 \div (-8)$ **3.** $-84 \div (-12)$ **4.** $120 \div 12$

In Exercises 5–12, find the quotient.

5. $45 \div (-9)$ **6.** $-35 \div (-7)$ **7.** $-144 \div 12$ **8.** $0 \div (-8)$

9. $64 \div (-16)$ **10.** $-48 \div (-6)$ **11.** $99 \div (-33)$ **12.** $54 \div (-9)$

In Exercises 13–15, find the average.

13. Yards gained or loss during a football game: –8, 5, 3, 2, –12

14. Gains or losses in college enrollment: 150, –50, 125, –75, 25

15. Depths of five small lakes: –52 ft, –35 ft, –12 ft, –24 ft, –32 ft

In Exercises 16–19, evaluate the expression when $x = -9$ and when $x = 9$.

16. $x + 4$ **17.** $10 + x$ **18.** $9 \div x$ **19.** $x \div (-3)$

In Exercises 20–22, evaluate the expression.

20. $(-4 + 25) \div (-3)$ **21.** $-6 \times (24 \div (-8))$ **22.** $(15 \times (-2)) \div (-3 \times (-2))$

23. The table shows the daily low temperature for a town in Montana for the first week in January. What is the average low temperature for the week?

Day	Sun	Mon	Tues	Wed	Thurs	Fri	Sat
Temp	9° F	–2° F	–9° F	0° F	–1° F	–10° F	–8° F

In Exercises 1–8, evaluate the expression.

1. $(-3)^2$

2. -5^2

3. $-(-2)^3$

4. $3 \cdot (-4)^2$

5. $-(-8)^2 + 4$

6. $-4^2 + (-5)^2$

7. $(-2)^3 - (-3)^2$

8. $-6^2 - (-3)^3$

In Exercises 9–12, make a table of values for the equation. Use x-values of −3, −2, −1, 0, 1, 2, 3. Then plot the points in a coordinate plane and describe any patterns that you see.

9. $y = 4 \cdot x^2$

10. $y = x^2 + 2$

11. $y = 4 - x^2$

12. $y = -2 \cdot x^2$

In Exercises 13–17, complete the statement using <, >, or =.

13. $(-3)^2$? $(-2)^3$

14. -1^4 ? $(-1)^4$

15. $(-4)^2$? -2^4

16. $(-3)^4$? 9^2

17. -6^2 ? -7^2

18. -5^2 ? $(-5)^2$

In Exercises 19–22, use a calculator to evaluate the expression.

19. $-4(-3)^5$

20. $-6^3 + (-8)^3$

21. $(-9)^3 - 3^5$

22. $(-5)^4 - 3^6$

23. Suppose you throw a ball into the air with a velocity of 96 feet per second from a height of 4 feet. The height of the object above the ground can be found using the equation $d = -16 \cdot t^2 + 96 \cdot t + 4$, where d is the distance and t is the time since you threw the object. Make a table showing the height above ground and the time t. Use t-values 0 through 7 seconds. Explain your results.

In Exercises 1–4, write the power of ten as a whole number or as a fraction.

1. 10^4
2. 10^{-8}
3. 10^9
4. 10^{-12}

In Exercises 5–10, write the number in scientific notation.

5. 850,000
6. 19,520,000
7. 0.0253

8. 0.000085
9. 548,000,000,000
10. 0.0000000000984

In Exercises 11–13, write the number in scientific notation.

11. A light year, the distance light can travel in one year, is approximately 5,880,000,000,000 miles.

12. There were about 63,100,000 subscribers to ESPN in 1993.

13. The mass of one electron is approximately 0.0000000000000000000000000009 grams.

In Exercises 14–17, complete the statement using <, >, or =.

14. $0.00035 \boxed{?} 3.5 \times 10^{-3}$

15. $8.34 \times 10^9 \boxed{?} 845,000,000$

16. $0.00405 \boxed{?} 4.5 \times 10^{-3}$

17. $508,000,000 \boxed{?} 5.08 \times 10^8$

In Exercises 18 and 19, choose the correct number.

18. The number of molecules in a drop of water

  a. 3.3×10^{19}
  b. 3.3×10^{-2}

19. The amount of iron in pounds in an average 150-pound person

  a. 6.0×10^3
  b. 6.0×10^{-3}

In Exercises 1–4, use the following information. A type of flower has genes that can produce 2 colors of petals: red (RR, Rr, and rR) and white (rr). Describe the plant parents and describe the probability of getting offspring with different colors of petals.

1.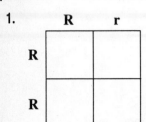

2.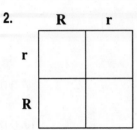

3.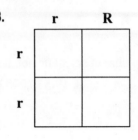

4.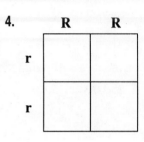

5. Color the spinner so that it has indicated probabilities.

   Red: $\frac{1}{6}$ Yellow: $\frac{1}{18}$ Blue: $\frac{4}{9}$ Green: $\frac{1}{3}$

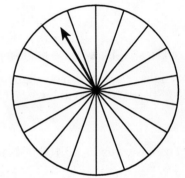

6. You and six of your friends are staying for one week at a cabin in a state park. The cabin has three sets of bunk beds and one single bed. The group decides that you will take turns sleeping in the single bed. To decide who goes first, you roll two number cubes. The first person to roll a sum of seven gets the single the first night. Draw a table showing the 36 possible outcomes. Then determine the probability of rolling a "seven".

7. You and some friends go to a carnival. You are trying to win a stuffed animal by pitching pennies into a tall glass having a small radius. You have pitched 40 pennies and 5 have made it in the glass. What is the probability that the next penny falls into the glass?

In Exercises 8–10, use the figure at the right. It shows the results of a survey of 500 adults who had worn Halloween costumes. Each person was asked how he or she acquired the costume.

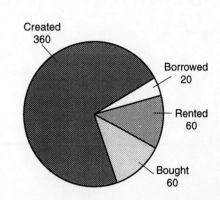

8. What is the probability that the person rented it?

9. What is the probability that the person did not buy it?

10. What is the probability that the person rented or bought it?

1. Copy and complete the tree diagram below. Then write a real-life problem that can be represented by the diagram.

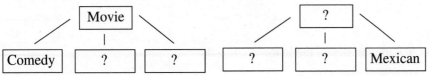

2. The four officers of a seventh grade class, Sue, David, Angel, and Brett, are having their picture taken for the yearbook. Use a tree diagram to determine the number of different ways the four can stand in a row.

3. Your dog has eaten almost all of the piece of paper that has your friend's new phone number since she moved. You can still see that the first three numbers are 339 and the last two numbers are 11. With this information, how many different numbers are possible? What is the probability of correctly guessing the correct number?

In Exercises 4 and 5, use the following information. You are on a game show. You have a chance to win a BRAND NEW CAR! All that you have to do is to guess the actual price of the car. The price is a five digit number. The diagram gives the choices for each digit.

				9
			3	0
		7	4	8
	4	5	7	4
2	5	0	9	2
1	3	2	8	1

4. How many possible prices are there?

5. What is the probability of randomly choosing the actual price on your initial guess?

In Exercises 6–8, use the following information. On a particular night at Luigi's Restaurant, there is a special in which you can have a dinner consisting of a cup of soup, one entree, one dessert, and a beverage for only $6.95. There are 4 kinds of soup, 10 entrees, 6 desserts and 3 different beverages.

6. How many different meals are possible?

7. Due to the competition of other restaurants, Luigi adds a choice of 5 types of salads for the same price. How many different meals are now available?

8. Luigi decides that he is losing too much money. So he reduces the number of entrees to only 5. Predict how many different meals are now available including the salads in Exercise 7. Explain your prediction. Check your answer by calculating the number of meals.

In Exercises 1–4, evaluate the expression.

1. 4!   2. 9!   3. 6!   4. 11!

In Exercises 5 and 6, find the number of permutations of the following objects. Then list the permutations to check your answer.

5.

6.

In Exercises 7 and 8, find the number of permutations of the letters in each word. Then list the permutations to check your answer. How many of the permutations are words?

7. RAT   8. POTS

9. There are 6 books each with different titles sitting in a pile on the floor. What is the probability that the books are piled in alphabetical order from top to bottom?

10. Sabrina's zip code consists of the numbers 1, 6, 8, 3, and 0. How many different zip codes are possible with these numbers? What is the probability that you randomly choose the correct zip code?

11. There are 7 horses in a horse race. What is the probability that you correctly pick the order that the horses finish the race?

12. You are working at a concession stand for the summer. The stand is very busy. There are four orders for hot dogs. When the hot dogs are finally ready, you forgot who was first, who was second as so on. What is the probability that you serve the customers in the correct order?

| **Practice** | **11.4** | Name _____ |

In Exercises 1–3, make a table like the one in Example 1 in your text book to count the number of combinations.

1. Choose 2 people from 5.   2. Choose 3 people from 6.   3. Choose 4 people from 5.

In Exercises 4–6, list the combinations.

4. Choose two symbols from the set { ★, ■ , ● }.

5. Choose three colors from the set {red, blue, green, white}.

6. Choose two numbers from the set { 0, 2, 4, 6}.

7. Use the figure at the right. There are five points labeled A-E. How many different triangles can be formed having their vertices at three of the five points? List them.

8. Six churches form a softball league. If each team must play every other team twice during the season, what is the total number of league games played?

A•

E•   • B

D •   • C

In Exercises 9–12, decide whether you need to find the number of permutations or combinations. Then find the answer.

9. In how many ways can your coach make a batting line-up for your baseball team with the nine players on your team?

10. How many ways can your class pick 2 classmates from 8 to present a report for the entire group?

11. A shipment of 10 CD players to a certain electronics store contained two players that do not work. If you purchased two CD players as birthday gifts for friends, determine the probability that both are defective.

12. There are seven books sitting on a shelf. Three of the books are autobiographies and four of the books are science fiction. Find the probability that when you pick 3 books from the 7 on the shelf that all 3 of the books are autobiographies?

In Exercises 1–3, is the spinner fair? If not, which color is most likely to win?

1.
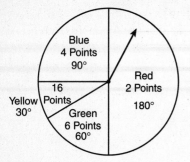

2.
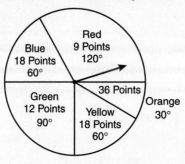

3.
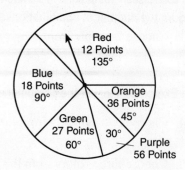

In Exercises 4-6, find the expected value of playing the game. Show your calculations.

4. A six sided cube has 3 green sides, 2 red sides and 1 blue side. The point values are as follows: blue = 6 points, red = 3 points and green = 2 points. The cube is rolled once.

5. Eight marbles are placed in a black velvet bag. Six of the marbles are black, 2 are white. A black marble is worth 0 points and a white marble is worth 5 points. One marble is drawn from the bag.

6. A game involves a tossing three coins. The player gets 10 points for 3 heads, 5 points for 2 heads, 1 point for 1 head, and no points for no heads. The coins are tossed once.

In Exercises 7 and 8, determine whether the game is fair. If the game is not fair which player is most likely to win? Explain.

7. Ginger and David are playing a game of straws. There are two short straws and 4 long straws in a group of 6 straws. If Ginger draws a short straw then she receives 10 points, and if she draws a long straw, then David receives 5 points. The first one to reach 100 wins the game.

8. Brett and Sue are playing a game with marbles. There are 24 marbles remaining in the bag. There are 11 red, 4 yellow, 3 purple, 4 orange, and 2 blue marbles still in the bag. Brett picks one marble, and if it is not red he receives 12 points. If it is red then Sue receives 15 points. The first one to reach 50 wins the game.

Practice

11.6

Name _____

In Exercises 1–3, predict the number of times that the event will occur if the experiment is performed 500 times.

1. Toss 3 coins. How many times will there be exactly 2 tails?

2. Toss 2 number cubes. How many times will you roll an even sum?

3. Choose a marble from a bag in which there are 6 red marbles and 4 blue marbles and 2 green marbles. Replace the marble. How many times will you choose a blue marble?

In Exercises 4 and 5, use the table at the right. It shows the area of the seven continents of the world.

Continent	Area (millions of square miles)
Africa	11.7
Antarctica	5.1
Asia	17.2
Australia	3.0
Europe	4.1
North America	9.4
South America	6.9

4. You throw a dart at a map of the world and it lands on land. What is the probability that it landed on a country in Europe?

5. If you throw a dart at the map and it lands on land 500 times, how many times would you predict that it landed on North America?

6. Complete the table by rolling a number cube and recording the number of times you roll a multiple of 2.

Number of rolls, x	10	20	30	40	50	60
Multiples of 2, y						

In Exercises 7–10, use the table in Exercise 6.

7. Write the data in the table as ordered pairs of the form (x, y). Then graph the ordered pairs in a coordinate plane.

8. Compute the number of times, k, you would expect to roll a multiple of 2 when you roll the number cube 60 times.

9. Draw a line that goes through the origin and through the point $(60, k)$, where k is the value found in Exercise 8.

10. Count the points that were over the prediction (above the line) and the number of points that were under the prediction (below the line).

Name _____

In Exercises 1–4, use the Venn diagram at the right to find the probability.

1. A or B, but not C

2. A, but not B or C

3. A or C, but not B

4. A, B, and C

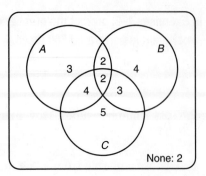

None: 2

In Exercises 5-8, write a statement represented by the Venn diagram.

5.

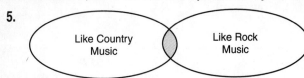

Like Country Music   Like Rock Music

6.

Enjoys Riding a Bike   Doesn't Enjoy Riding a Bike

7.

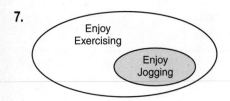

Enjoy Exercising

Enjoy Jogging

8.

Pizza Eaters

Pepperoni   Sausage

In Exercises 9–13, use the following information. A survey asked 40 students in a class if they own CD's, cassettes or albums. Of the 40 asked, 15 own only CD's, 12 own only cassettes, none own only albums, 10 own both CD's and cassettes, 3 own all three types. Sketch a Venn diagram and use it to find the probability if one student was selected at random, he or she:

9. owns CD's only

10. owns cassettes only

11. owns albums only

12. owns both CD's and cassettes

13. owns all three types

Practice   **12.1**   Name _____

In Exercises 1–4, name the inverse operation.

1. Subtract 8   **2.** Add −5   **3.** Multiply by 2   **4.** Divide by −6

In Exercises 5–12, complete the box model.

5.

6.

7.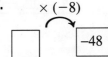

8.

9.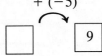

10.

11.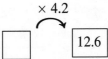

12.

In Exercises 13–18, write a box model for the equation. Then use an inverse operation to solve the equation.

13. $e + 8 = -2$ **14.** $w - 15 = 3$ **15.** $-12r = -48$

16. $s - (-14) = 26$ **17.** $j \div 9 = -2$ **18.** $q \cdot 15 = -45$

In Exercises 19–22, write an equation that represents the box model. Then solve the equation.

19.

20.

21.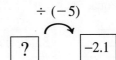

22.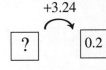

In Exercises 1–3, determine whether $q = -5$ is a solution.

1. $-5 - q = -10$

2. $q - 5 = 0$

3. $q - (-5) = 0$

In Exercises 4–6, rewrite the equation in a simpler form. Then solve the equation.

4. $e + (-15) = 20$

5. $-20 = w - (-12)$

6. $t - (-10) = 20$

In Exercises 7–9, write an addition equation to find the side length or the angle measure labeled x. Then solve the equation and check your solution.

7. Perimeter = 22

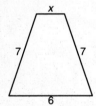

8.

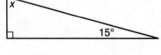

9. Perimeter = 40

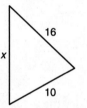

In Exercises 10–12, solve the equation. Then check your solution.

10. $w - \frac{2}{5} = \frac{1}{2}$

11. $-15.2 = f - (-2.6)$

12. $-\frac{11}{8} = t + \frac{3}{4}$

13. With the 1.2-inch rainfall today, the total for the month is 4.5 inches. How much rain had been recorded for the month before today? Use the model below to write an equation. Then solve the equation.

| Rainfall today | + | Rainfall before today | = | Rainfall for the month |

14. The sale price of a new pair of cross-trainers is $74.96. If the discount is $24.99, what was the original price? Use the model below to write an equation. Then solve the equation.

| Original price | − | Discount | = | Sale price |

12.3

Name _____

In Exercises 1–4, without solving the equation decide whether the solution is positive or negative. Then solve the equation.

1. $6d = -30$

2. $48 = 12r$

3. $-8t = -64$

4. $-4w = 30$

In Exercises 5–12, use mental math to estimate the solution of the equation. Then solve the equation.

5. $3q = 46$

6. $51 = 5g$

7. $-12e = 26$

8. $-32 = -3f$

9. $2.5p = -12$

10. $-5.2x = -26$

11. $9w = -3.6$

12. $12s = 7.2$

In Exercises 13–20, solve the equation.

13. $4f = 48$

14. $-45 = 3d$

15. $-3g = 0$

16. $14.4 = -6q$

17. $12a = 15$

18. $-17p = 102$

19. $-29.4 = -9.8a$

20. $6.2z = 23.56$

In Exercises 21–23, write an equation represented by the verbal sentence. Then solve the equation.

21. A number multiplied by −4 is 24.

22. −32 is 6.4 times a number.

23. The product of −7 and a number is −119.

24. You are traveling with your parents to the mountains for the week-end. The cabin at which you are staying is about 203 miles from your hometown. If you think that you can average 58 miles per hour for the entire trip, about how long will it take to arrive? Use the model below to write an equation. Then solve the equation.

| Distance | = | Rate of travel | × | Travel time |

In Exercises 1–4, decide whether the solution is positive or negative without solving the equation.

1. $\dfrac{e}{7} = -3$

2. $q \div -6 = -4$

3. $\dfrac{z}{-8} = 2$

4. $d \div 21 = 4$

In Exercises 5–13, solve the equation. Then check your solution.

5. $\dfrac{e}{5} = 6$

6. $\dfrac{t}{-6} = -3$

7. $s \div 15 = -3$

8. $\dfrac{w}{1.5} = 2$

9. $a \div \dfrac{2}{3} = \dfrac{3}{4}$

10. $\dfrac{y}{2.5} = -10.5$

11. $k \div -4 = 16.4$

12. $\dfrac{m}{-5.6} = -5.5$

13. $b \div 2.4 = 8.4$

In Exercises 14–16, write a division equation to find the area of the figure. Then solve the equation and check your solution.

14.
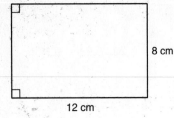
8 cm

12 cm

15.
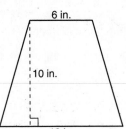
6 in.

10 in.

12 in.

16.

6 mi

4 mi

17. In order to measure the height of the twin towers of the World Trade Center in New York City, suppose you use the following plan. You measure the shadow cast by one of the buildings and find it to be 340.5 feet. Then you measure the shadow cast by a 4-foot post and find that it is 1 foot long. Use the verbal model below to write an equation to estimate the height of the World Trade Center towers. Then solve that equation.

$$\dfrac{\text{Height of tower}}{\text{Length of shadow}} = \dfrac{\text{Height of post}}{\text{Length of shadow}}$$

Practice

12.5

Name _____

In Exercises 1–3, describe the first step you would use to solve the equation.

1. $2x + 5 = -3$

2. $-15 + 3d = 3$

3. $\dfrac{w}{8} - 5 = 1$

In Exercises 4–6, write the equation represented by the box model. Then solve the equation and check the solution using the box model.

4.

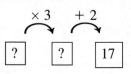

5.

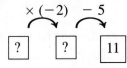

6.

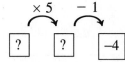

In Exercises 7–14, solve the equation. Then check the solution.

7. $11 + 3m = -1$

8. $-5x + 7 = -3$

9. $\dfrac{b}{4} - 2 = 1$

10. $8w - 6 = 6$

11. $-15 = 8c - 15$

12. $\dfrac{t}{16} + \dfrac{1}{8} = \dfrac{3}{4}$

13. $2q - \dfrac{1}{2} = \dfrac{3}{2}$

14. $2.6 + 4r = 9.2$

In Exercises 15 and 16, solve the equation. Then use the solution to find the angle measures.

15. $13x + 11 = 180$

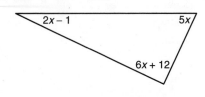

16. $23x - 8 = 360$

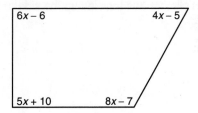

17. You are at the beach enjoying the ocean. You saw two different stands that rent bikes by the hour. One stand, Beachbum's, charges a fee of $16 plus $2 per hour. Another stand, Waverunner's charges $10 plus $3 per hour. You want to rent as long as possible and have $40 to spend. Use the verbal model below for each stand and solve the resulting equation. From which stand would you rent? Explain your reasoning.

| Cost per hour | × | Number of hours | + | One-time fee | = | Amount to spend |

In Exercises 1–4, make an input-output table for the function. Use *x*-values of 1, 2, 3, 4, 5, and 6.

1. $y = 3x + 5$

2. $y = \dfrac{x}{2} - 1$

3. $y = -5x + 5$

4. $y = 4(x + 2)$

In Exercises 5–8, use the input-output table to write an equation for the function.

5.

Input, x	1	2	3	4	5	6
Output, y	1	3	5	7	9	11

6.

Input, x	1	2	3	4	5	6
Output, y	2	1	0	-1	-2	-3

7.

Input, x	1	2	3	4	5	6
Output, y	4	9	14	19	24	29

8.

Input, x	1	2	3	4	5	6
Output, y	1.5	2	2.5	3	3.5	4

In Exercises 9 and 10, use the graph at the right. It shows the number of feet *n* that a mountain climber has traveled up the side of a 300 foot cliff after climbing for *t* hours.

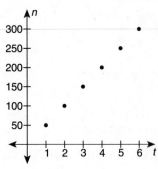

9. Make a table of the input t and the output n.

10. Write an equation that represents the number of feet climbed in t hours.

In Exercises 11 and 12, use the following information. You are joining a video rental club, MOO-V's. They charge an annual fee of $5 plus $1.50 per movie.

11. Make a table of the cost c for one year of renting n movies. Use input values of 10, 20, 30, 40, and 50 movies.

12. Write a function that represents the cost of renting n movies for one year.

Answers to Practice Workbook

■ Lesson 1.1

1.

	Width	Length	Area
Original	2	3	6
Doubled	4	6	24
Tripled	6	9	54
Quadrupled	8	12	96

When the dimensions are doubled, the area increases by a factor of 4. When the dimensions are tripled, the area increases by a factor of 9. Finally, when the dimensions are quadrupled, the area increases by a factor of 16. The extra rectangle varies.

2. Yes, if you round the prices to the nearest dollar, the total is only $24.

3. 9 different cakes; white cake with white, chocolate, or lemon frosting; chocolate cake with white, chocolate, or lemon frosting; yellow cake with white, chocolate, or lemon frosting

4. The type which is $2.50 for 5 pounds is the better bargain, because it costs $0.50 per pound, while the other type costs about $0.58 per pound.

■ Lesson 1.2

1. 29; each number can be found by adding 6 to the previous number.

2. 22; each number can be found by adding the next even integer to the preceding number.

3.

Number	1	2	3	4	5
Triangular	1	3	6	10	15
Square	1	4	9	16	25

The nth square number is n^2. The nth square number is also the sum of the nth triangular number and the $(n-1)$th triangular number. The 20th square number is $20^2 = 400$, which is also equal to the sum of the 19th and 20th triangular numbers; $190 + 210 = 400$.

4. 10; count the triangles.

5. $20 \times 18 = 360$ different dance couples are possible. The strategy is to use the Basic Counting Principle.

■ Lesson 1.3

1.–4. Sketches vary.

5. Perimeter: 36 in.; Area: 72 sq in.

6. Perimeter: 36 ft; Area: 54 sq ft

7. Perimeter: 20 m; Area: 25 sq m

8. Perimeter: 30 cm; Area: 30 sq cm

9. Perimeter: 40 in.; Area: 80 sq. in.

10. Perimeter: 66 ft; Area: 240 sq ft

11. Perimeter: 100 mm; Area: 600 sq mm

12. Yes   **13.** Yes   **14.** No   **15.** No

16. **17.**

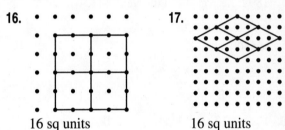

16 sq units   16 sq units

18.

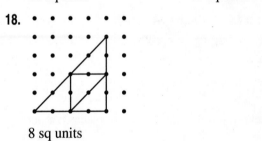

8 sq units

■ Lesson 1.4

1. Since there are 4 possible outcomes; BB, BG, GB, GG, approximately 25 out of 100 couples having 2 children would have 2 boys. Results from the experiments vary.

2. A 6-sided number cube experiment might be the best simulation. Perform the experiment a number of times and find the average of the number of tosses it takes to get a repeat.

3. A 6-sided number cube experiment might be the best simulation. Perform the experiment a number of times and find the average of the number of tosses it takes to get all 6 numbers.

4. If the actual coins are not available, 12 quarters could be used and 4 quarters could be designated as the real quarters. Another possibility is use different colored marbles in a bag with a certain color of marble designated as the quarters. Results vary.

■ Lesson 1.5

1.

8	3	4
1	5	9
6	7	2

2.

2	7	6
9	5	1
4	3	8

3.

5	0	7
6	4	2
1	8	3

4. 21   **5.** 31   **6.** 52

7. 20   **8.** 40   **9.** 18 and 18

10. Sue is 40 years old and Rachel is 10 years old.

11. 1892; he was 44 in the year 44^2, which is 1936.

■ Lesson 1.6

1. Yes   **2.** Yes   **3.** No   **4.** Yes

5. No   **6.** Yes   **7.** 20   **8.** 12

9. 17   **10.** 8   **11.** 7   **12.** 4

13. $x + 12 = 36$, $x = 24$

14. $26 - x = 12$, $x = 14$

15. $7 \times t = 49$, $t = 7$ **16.** $\frac{k}{11} = 4$, $k = 44$

17. 4.31   **18.** 2.6   **19.** 5.25

20. Let p represent the number of pieces per person.

$\frac{52}{p} = 4$, $p = 13$

■ Lesson 1.7

1.
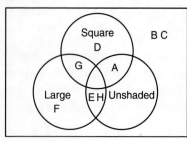

2.
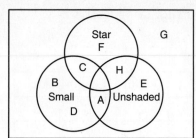

3.
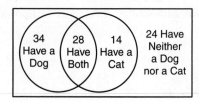

4. Mary, Harry, Larry, and Sherry

5. Brett likes the 49ers. Gabrielle likes the Cowboys. Sue likes the Bengals, and Jose likes the Panthers.

6. 28 children said that they have both a dog and a cat.

■ Lesson 1.8

1. 9 different combinations: 12, 2 + 10, 4 + 8, 6 + 6, 2 + 4 + 6, 2 + 2 + 8, 4 + 4 + 4, 2 + 2 + 2 + 6, 2 + 2 + 4 + 4

2. 6 different ways:
  1. Maria, Pierre, Jackelyn
  2. Maria, Jackelyn, Pierre
  3. Pierre, Maria, Jackelyn
  4. Pierre, Jackelyn, Maria
  5. Jackelyn, Maria, Pierre
  6. Jackelyn, Pierre, Maria

3.   **4.**

5. 6 different ways: 1 quarter and 1 dime, 1 quarter and 2 nickels, 3 dimes and 1 nickel, 2 dimes and 3 nickels, 1 dime and 5 nickels, or 7 nickels

6. 2

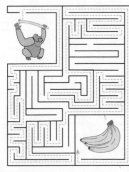

7. 5 different ways: 9 dozen nightcrawlers,
1 dozen minnows and 7 dozen nightcrawlers,
2 dozen minnows and 5 dozen nightcrawlers,
3 dozen minnows and 3 dozen nightcrawlers,
or 4 dozen minnows and 1 dozen nightcrawlers

■ **Lesson 1.9**

1. 7 stuffed animals; strategy: working backwards

2. 6 years old; strategy: Guess, Check, Revise

3. 24; strategy: making a list   **4.** 9

5. Since 1975, the number of hospitals is
decreasing. Reasons vary.

■ **Lesson 2.1**

1. Error: subtraction was performed before
division. $16 - \frac{4}{2} = 16 - 2 = 14$

2. Error: addition was performed before division.
$\frac{15}{3} + 2 = 5 + 2 = 7$

3. 3   **4.** 17   **5.** 20   **6.** 4   **7.** 1

8. 24   **9.** 2   **10.** 18   **11.** 15

12. False; $\frac{14}{(7 - 5)} = 7$ **13.** True

14. False; $\frac{(25 + 15)}{5} = 8$

15. False; $24 - 4 \times (2 + 2) = 8$ **16.** True

17. False; $\frac{10 \times 8}{(2 + 6)} = 10$

18. $15 \times 6 - 25 = 65$ **19.** $21 + \frac{144}{16} = 30$

20. $\frac{12.5}{2} - 5 = 1.25$

21. $30.5 \times 2 + 3.4 = 64.4$

■ **Lesson 2.2**

1. 4^5 **2.** d^4 **3.** e^6 **4.** 8   **5.** 1000

6. 16   **7.** 9   **8.** 125   **9.** 1   **10.** 16

11. 64   **12.** 64   **13.** n^3 **14.** $2 \times n^3$

15. $8 \times n^3$ **16.** 18; 135   **17.** 4; 100

18. 10; 52   **19.** 15; 624   **20.** 25; 64

21. $8; \frac{1}{2}$ **22.** >   **23.** =   **24.** >

25. <   **26.** =   **27.** =

■ **Lesson 2.3**

1. Always; examples vary.

2. Sometimes; examples are multiplies of 10.

3. Sometimes; examples are even numbers that
are also divisible by 9.

4. 315 is divisible by 3, 5, and 9.

5. 600 is divisible by 2, 3, 4, 5, 6, and 10.

6. 852 is divisible by 2, 3, 4, and 6.

7. 1024 is divisible by 2 and 4.

8. 8505 is divisible by 3, 5, and 9.

9. 6360 is divisible by 2, 3, 4, 5, 6, and 10.

10. 12,548 is divisible by 2 and 4.

11. 130,680 is divisible by 2, 3, 4, 5, 6, 9, and 10.

12. 4   **13.** 8   **14.** 1   **15.** 3

16.

	24

$$1 \boxed{}$$

2 \boxed{12}   4 \boxed{6}

3 \boxed{8}

17.

$$1 \boxed{} \; 56$$

2 \boxed{28}   7 \boxed{8}

4 \boxed{14}

18.

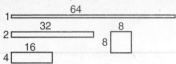

19.

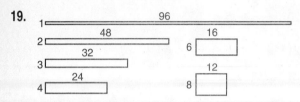

20. a. yes; b. yes; c. yes; d. no; e. no; f. yes
Leap years occur when the year number is divisible by 4. The only exception is the first year of a new century which is only a leap year if it is divisible by 400, i.e. 2000.

■ Lesson 2.4

1.–3. Trees vary.

1. $2^2 \cdot 3^2$ **2.** $2^3 \cdot 3^2$

3. $2^2 \cdot 3^2 \cdot 5$ **4.** $2^5 \cdot 3^2 \cdot 7$

5. $2^3 \cdot 5^2 \cdot 7$ **6.** $2^4 \cdot 3^3 \cdot 5$

7. 50   **8.** 42   **9.** 108   **10.** 180

11. 200   **12.** 1260   **13.** 23, prime

14. 29, prime   **15.** 21, composite

16. 26; the sum of prime factors is 15.

17. 47; the sum of the prime factors of 48 is 11.

18. 11, 13, 17, 37, 79

■ Lesson 2.5

1. c   **2.** a   **3.** d   **4.** b

5. Factors of 15: 1, 3, 5, 15
Factors of 27: 1, 3, 9, 27
Greatest Common Factor: 3

6. Factors of 12: 1, 2, 3, 4, 6, 12
Factors of 42: 1, 2, 3, 6, 7, 14, 21, 42
Greatest Common Factor: 6

7. Factors of 45: 1, 3, 5, 9, 15, 45
Factors of 63: 1, 3, 7, 9, 21, 63
Greatest Common Factor: 9

8. Factors of 48: 1, 2, 3, 4, 6, 8, 12, 16, 24, 48
Factors of 64: 1, 2, 4, 8, 16, 32, 64
Greatest Common Factor: 16

9.–12. Answers and methods vary.

13. 6   **14.** 5   **15.** 24

16. 1-by-1, 4320 patches; 2-by-2, 1080 patches 3-by-3, 480 patches; 4-by-4, 270 patches 6-by-6, 120 patches; 12-by-12, 30 patches The 12-by-12 patches require the least number of patches, 30.

■ Lesson 2.6

1.–4. Answers vary.

5. $\frac{5}{6}$ **6.** $\frac{1}{2}$ **7.** $\frac{1}{4}$ **8.** $\frac{2}{3}$ **9.** $\frac{2}{5}$

10. $\frac{5}{9}$ **11.** $\frac{3}{5} = \frac{15}{25} = \frac{18}{30}$ **12.** $\frac{45}{63} = \frac{10}{14} = \frac{5}{7}$

13. $\frac{28}{32} = \frac{14}{16} = \frac{21}{24} = \left(\frac{7}{8}\right)$ **14.** $\frac{16}{24} = \frac{20}{30} = \frac{2}{3}$

15. $\frac{4}{25}$; other fractions vary.

16. $\frac{2}{3}$; other fractions vary.

17. $\frac{3}{4}$; other fractions vary.   **18.** $\frac{3}{20}$ **19.** $\frac{9}{50}$

20. $\frac{1}{10}$ **21.** $\frac{1}{8}$ **22.** $\frac{11}{40}$ **23.** $\frac{9}{100}$ **24.** $\frac{2}{25}$

■ Lesson 2.7

1. $\frac{75}{100}$; 0.75   **2.** $\frac{80}{100}$; 0.8   **3.** $\frac{64}{100}$; 0.64

4. $\frac{55}{100}$; 0.55   **5.** 0.63   **6.** 0.17   **7.** 0.58

8. 0.33   **9.** 0.44   **10.** 0.22   **11.** 0.51

12. 0.47

13. $0.\overline{12}, 0.\overline{15}, 0.\overline{18}$; the decimals are increasing by $0.\overline{03}$.

14. $0.\overline{27}, 0.\overline{28}, 0.\overline{29}$; the decimals have a repeating pattern that is the same as the numerator of the fraction.

15. $\frac{1}{100}$ **16.** $\frac{1}{2}$ **17.** $\frac{1}{9}$ **18.** $\frac{1}{50}$

19. $\frac{21}{100}$; 0.21   **20.** $\frac{4}{25}$; 0.16   **21.** $\frac{1}{20}$; 0.05

22. $\frac{1}{20}$; 0.05   **23.** $\frac{1}{25}$; 0.04   **24.** $\frac{1}{50}$; 0.02

■ Lesson 2.8

1. $a = \frac{7}{4}$, $b = \frac{9}{4}$, $\frac{9}{4} > \frac{7}{4}$ or $\frac{7}{4} < \frac{9}{4}$

2. $a = \frac{33}{10}$, $b = \frac{17}{4}$, $\frac{17}{4} > \frac{33}{10}$ or $\frac{33}{10} < \frac{17}{4}$

3.

2.5, 3.05, 3.45, 3.95, 4.25, 4.75

4.

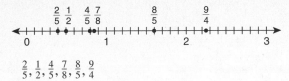

$\frac{2}{5}, \frac{1}{2}, \frac{4}{5}, \frac{7}{8}, \frac{8}{5}, \frac{9}{4}$

5.

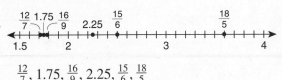

$\frac{12}{7}, 1.75, \frac{16}{9}, 2.25, \frac{15}{6}, \frac{18}{5}$

6.

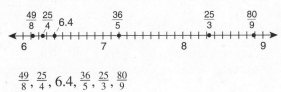

$\frac{49}{8}, \frac{25}{4}, 6.4, \frac{36}{5}, \frac{25}{3}, \frac{80}{9}$

7.

The list starts at $\frac{1}{4}$ or 0.25 and the next number is 0.4 or $\frac{2}{5}$ more than the preceding number. The next 2 numbers are 2.25 or $\frac{9}{4}$ and 2.65 or $\frac{53}{20}$.

8.

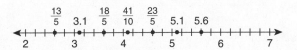

The list starts at $\frac{13}{5}$ or 2.6 and the next number is 0.5 or $\frac{1}{2}$ more than the preceding number. The next 2 numbers are 5.1 or $\frac{51}{10}$ and 5.6 or $\frac{28}{5}$.

9.

10.

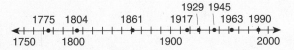

■ Lesson 3.1

1. 3: 3, 6, 9, 12, 15, 18, 21, 24, 27, 30;
10: 10, 20, 30, 40, 50, 60, 70, 80, 90, 100;
LCM: 30

2. 2: 2, 4, 6, 8, 10, 12, 14, 16, 18, 20;
9: 9, 18, 27, 36, 45, 54, 63, 72, 81, 90;
LCM: 18

3. 4: 4, 8, 12, 16, 20, 24, 28, 32, 36, 40;
18: 18, 36, 54, 72, 90, 108, 126, 144, 162, 180;
LCM: 36

4. 12: 12, 24, 36, 48, 60, 72, 84, 96, 108, 120;
16: 16, 32, 48, 64, 80, 96, 112, 128, 144, 160;
LCM: 48

5. 2: 2, 4, 6, 8, 10, 12, 14, 16, 18, 20;
3: 3, 6, 9, 12, 15, 18, 21, 24, 27, 30;
6: 6, 12, 18, 24, 30, 36, 42, 48, 54, 60;
LCM: 6

6. 3: 3, 6, 9, 12, 15, 18, 21, 24, 27, 30;
4: 4, 8, 12, 16, 20, 24, 28, 32, 36, 40;
8: 8, 16, 24, 32, 40, 48, 56, 64, 72, 80;
LCM: 24

7. 96   **8.** 315   **9.** 144   **10.** 990

11. 70   **12.** 60   **13.** 10, 15; LCM: 30

14. 12, 18; LCM: 36   **15.** 14, 21; LCM: 42

16. Yes, every 24 days; May 24, June 17, July 11, Aug. 4, Aug. 28, and Sept. 21.

■ Lesson 3.2

1. Proper; less than 1.   **2.** Improper; more than 1.

3. Improper; more than 1.

4. Proper; less than 1.   **5.** b   **6.** c

7. d   **8.** a   **9.** $6\frac{1}{2}$ **10.** $2\frac{5}{7}$ **11.** $3\frac{1}{4}$

12. $7\frac{4}{5}$ **13.** $\frac{15}{8}$ **14.** $\frac{27}{11}$ **15.** $\frac{77}{9}$

16. $\frac{37}{3}$ **17.** 3.6   **18.** 6.25   **19.** 3.7

20. 5.6   **21.** 1.875   **22.** 3.4375

23. 5.15   **24.** 4.36   **25.** True

26. False; it is equal to forty-two tenths.

■ Lesson 3.3

1. $\frac{4}{5}$ **2.** $\frac{2}{11}$ **3.** $\frac{22}{15}$ **4.** $\frac{13}{21}$ **5.** $\frac{31}{45}$

6. $\frac{1}{30}$ **7.** $\frac{4}{3}$ **8.** $\frac{23}{24}$ **9.** $\frac{17}{32}, \frac{9}{16}, \frac{5}{8}, \frac{3}{4}, \frac{2}{2}$

10. $\frac{9}{14}, \frac{11}{14}, \frac{13}{14}, \frac{15}{14}, \frac{17}{14}$ **11.** $\frac{5}{24}, \frac{4}{20}, \frac{3}{16}, \frac{2}{12}, \frac{1}{8}$

12. $\frac{3}{5}$ **13.** $\frac{6}{11}$ **14.** $\frac{1}{3}$ **15.** $\frac{3}{8}$ **16.** $\frac{7}{12}$

17. $\frac{3}{10}$

18. Jerri weighed $\frac{1}{16}$ of a pound more than Joseph.

19. You ran further by $\frac{1}{40}$ of a mile.

■ **Lesson 3.4**

1. $4\frac{2}{5}$ **2.** $6\frac{2}{3}$ **3.** $3\frac{1}{4}$ **4.** $11\frac{1}{3}$

5. $7\frac{2}{3}$ **6.** $10\frac{5}{8}$ **7.** $1\frac{3}{7}$ **8.** $2\frac{1}{2}$

9. $5\frac{7}{12}$ **10.** $2\frac{7}{15}$ **11.** $7\frac{9}{16}$ **12.** $1\frac{5}{12}$

13. $3\frac{1}{2}$ feet   **14.** $3\frac{1}{20}$ yards   **15.** $9\frac{1}{2}$ feet

16. Monday: $\$49\frac{3}{8}$; Tuesday: $\$48\frac{5}{8}$;

Wednesday: $\$48\frac{3}{4}$; Thursday: $\$49\frac{1}{8}$;

Friday: $\$48\frac{7}{8}$

■ **Lesson 3.5**

1. $\frac{4}{7}$ **2.** $\frac{3}{4}$ **3.** 6   **4.** $10\frac{1}{2}$ **5.** $7\frac{4}{5}$

6. 20   **7.** $2\frac{5}{18}$ **8.** $3\frac{1}{2}$ **9.** $13\frac{7}{16}$

10. 22   **11.** $\frac{17}{48}$ **12.** $30\frac{1}{4}$ **13.** $5\frac{1}{16}$

14. $21\frac{1}{3}$ **15.** $15\frac{3}{10}$ **16.** 20 cups

17. Total laps: $11\frac{1}{4}$ laps; total miles: $4\frac{1}{2}$ miles

■ **Lesson 3.6**

1. $6(5 + 3) = 6 \cdot 5 + 6 \cdot 3$

2. $7(5 + 2) = 7 \cdot 5 + 7 \cdot 2$

3. 72   **4.** 168   **5.** 41   **6.** $4\frac{1}{3}$

7. $7\frac{1}{2}$ **8.** 13   **9.** $8t + 16$

10. $56 + 14f$ **11.** $11d$ **12.** $15e$

13. $2f + 2p$ **14.** $v + 9$

15. 33; they are equivalent expressions.

16. $23\frac{1}{2}$; they are equivalent expressions.

17. 63   **18.** 168   **19.** 203.2   **20.** 60.48

■ **Lesson 3.7**

1. b   **2.** d   **3.** a   **4.** c

5. $3\frac{2}{9}$ **6.** $2\frac{11}{80}$ **7.** $\frac{9}{16}$ **8.** $1\frac{61}{204}$

9. 4   **10.** $2\frac{26}{49}$ **11.** $2\frac{68}{125}$ **12.** $\frac{8}{31}$

13. $2\frac{9}{20}$ **14.** $1\frac{1}{4}$ **15.** $1\frac{17}{27}$ **16.** $1\frac{35}{48}$

17. $\frac{2}{3}$ **18.** $\frac{1}{3}$ **19.** $\frac{1}{2}$ **20.** 2   **21.** $\frac{1}{5}$

22. $\frac{4}{3}$ **23.** $\frac{5}{8} \div \frac{9}{4} = \frac{5}{18}$

24. $\frac{20}{3} \div \frac{32}{9} = \frac{15}{8} = 1\frac{7}{8}$

25. 18; $56\frac{1}{2} \div 3\frac{1}{8} = 18\frac{2}{25}$

■ **Lesson 4.1**

1.

x	1	2	3	4	5	6
$2x + 3$	5	7	9	11	13	15

2.

x	1	2	3	4	5	6
$x \div 2$	$\frac{1}{2}$	1	$\frac{3}{2}$	2	$\frac{5}{2}$	3

3.

x	1	2	3	4	5	6
$5 + 8x$	13	21	29	37	45	53

4.

x	1	2	3	4	5	6
$42 - 4x$	38	34	30	26	22	18

5.

y	1	2	3	4	5
$6y - 1$	5	11	17	23	29

6.

y	1	2	3	4	5
$22 - 2y$	20	18	16	14	12

7.

y	1	2	3	4	5
$7y + 4$	11	18	25	32	39

8. a.

n	1	2	3	4	5
Cost ($)	4	5	6	7	8

Cost: $n + 3$

b.

n	1	2	3	4	5
Cost ($)	9.50	11	12.50	14	15.50

Cost: $8 + 1.5n$

■ **Lesson 4.2**

1. (3, 2)   **2.** (1, 5)   **3.** (0, 4)   **4.** (3, 0)

5. (4, 2)   **6.** (2, 4)

7. (1, 1), (2, 3), (3, 5), (4, 7), (5, 9), (6, 11)

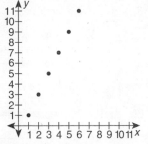

8. (1, 14), (2, 12), (3, 10), (4, 8), (5, 6), (6, 4)

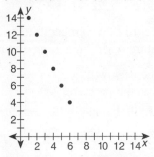

9.

x	1	2	3	4	5
y	5	7	9	11	13

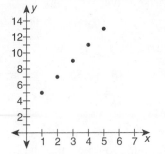

For every increase of 1 in x, there is an increase of 2 in y.

10.

x	1	2	3	4	5
y	15	12	9	6	3

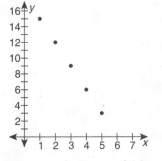

For every increase of 1 in x, there is a decrease of 3 in y.

11. Camp Waka-Waka

Children	1	2	3	4	5	6
Cost ($)	6	9	12	15	18	21

Camp Barking Spider

Children	1	2	3	4	5	6
Cost ($)	8	10	12	14	16	18

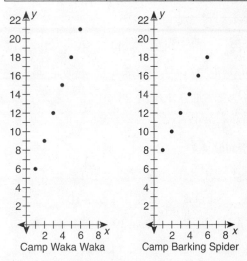

Camp Waka Waka   Camp Barking Spider

Camp Waka-Waka is cheaper for less than 3 children. Camp Barking Spider is cheaper for more than 3 children. The cost is the same for 3 children.

■ Lesson 4.3

1.

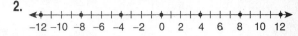

Each next number is 3 more than the preceding number; 8, 11.

2.

Each next number is 4 less than the preceding number; −8, −12.

3.

The difference between two consecutive numbers is increasing by 1 with each new number; −7, −13.

4.

Each number is found by adding the next odd integer to the preceding number; 15, 26.

5. <   **6.** <   **7.** >   **8.** >

9.

False; $-2 > -5$

10.

False; $-12 < -9$

11.

False

12. -12 **13.** 2820 **14.** -50 **15.** -12

16. 500 **17.** -2 **18.** $-8, -5, 0, 2, 4$

19. $-2.5, -1, 0, 1.02, 1.25$

20. $-4.5, -4.05, -\frac{5}{2}, -\frac{7}{4}, 2.5$

■ Lesson 4.4

1. $-3 + 4 = 1$ **2.** $2 + (-6) = -4$

3. 6 **4.** -4 **5.** 2 **6.** -10 **7.** 3

8. -4 **9.** 5 **10.** -39 **11.** b; -8

12. c; -2 **13.** a; 2 **14.** -2 **15.** -12

16. $5\frac{1}{3}$ **17.** Positive **18.** Zero

19. Negative **20.** -8 **21.** 5 **22.** -6

23. $-6 + 18 = 12°$ F

24. $-2 + (-13) = -15°$ F

■ Lesson 4.5

1. When you subtract a negative number, you should move to the right; $5 - (-3) = 8$.

2. When you subtract a positive number, you should move to the left; $-8 - 5 = -13$.

3. c **4.** b **5.** a

6.

7.

8.

9. 14 **10.** -13 **11.** -2 **12.** 30

13. 0 **14.** -44 **15.** 52 **16.** -50

17. 68 **18.** -146 **19.** 177 **20.** 620

21. -799 **22.** -18 **23.** 1331

24. -5 **25.** 2

■ Lesson 4.6

1. -13 **2.** 6 **3.** -5 **4.** -4 **5.** -1.1

6. $-\frac{1}{8}$ **7.** $-\frac{3}{16}$ **8.** -8.88 **9.** -64

10.–12. Equations vary.

13. $x + 4 = -5; -9$ **14.** $20 + x = -15; -35$

15. $-2 = 18 + x; -20$ **16.** $16 = x + 13; 3$

17. -283 **18.** -1387 **19.** -57.01

20. -0.015 **21.** 58.5 **22.** -165.8

23. Verbal Mode: Record Low Temperature + Rise in Temperature = Morning Temperature

Labels: Let x = record low.

15 = rise in temperature.

-8 = morning temperature.

Equation: $x + 15 = -8; x = -23°$ F

■ Lesson 4.7

1. Negative; -5 **2.** Negative; -8

3. Positive; 9 **4.–6.** Equations vary.

7. -1 **8.** 5 **9.** 32 **10.** 10 **11.** -30

12. -8 **13.** 6 **14.** $\frac{3}{10}$ **15.** 39

16. $3\frac{11}{12}$ **17.** 22.84 **18.** -9.85

19. $n - 12 = -12; 0$ **20.** $32 = n + 51; -19$

21. $-\frac{3}{8} = n - \frac{1}{6}; -\frac{5}{24}$

22. Verbal Model: Amount you gave the clerk − the cost of the hot dogs and freezy = the amount of change

Labels: Let x = the amount you gave the clerk.

1.78 = the cost of the food.

3.22 = the amount of change.

Equation: $x - 1.78 = 3.22; x = \$5$

■ Lesson 5.1

1. 4, 4, 5, 5, 6, 6, 7, 7, 8, 8, 8, 9, 10, 11; mean = 7, median = 7, mode = 8

2. 3.75, 3.75, 4.00, 4.25, 4.50, 5.00, 5.00, 5.25, 5.25, 5.50, 5.75, 5.75, 6.00, 6.25, 6.25, 6.25, 6.25, 6.50, 6.50, 7.00; mean = 5.44, median = 5.63, mode = 6.25

3. 1, 2, 3, 3, 3, 4, 5, 5, 7, 9, 10, 12, 14, 14, 15, 16, 18, 26, 30, 44; mean = 12.05, median = 9.5, mode = 3

4. 2, 2, 2, 2, 3, 3, 3, 3, 4, 4, 4, 4, 4, 4, 5, 5, 5, 5, 6, 6, 6, 8, 9, 10, 11; mean = 4.8, median = 4, mode = 4

5. Answers vary.   **6.** Answers vary.

7. Mean: 41.5, median: 37, mode: 37; for the data presented the median or the mode best represents the data. The data is centered about the median.

■ **Lesson 5.2**

1. The greatest: 20–24; the least 40–44

2. Statements vary.

3.

Number of foreign-born residents (thousands)	Tally	Frequency
0–49	⅀⅀ ⅀⅀ |||	18
50–99	⅀⅀ ⅀⅀	10
100–149	⅀⅀	5
150–199	||	2
200–249		0
250–299	|||	3
300–349	|||	3
350–399	||	2
400–449		0
450–499		0
500–549		0
550–599			1

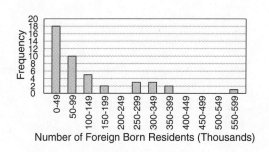

4.

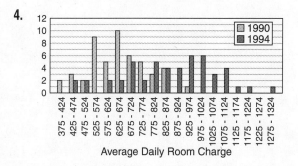

■ **Lesson 5.3**

1. c   **2.** d   **3.** a   **4.** b

5.

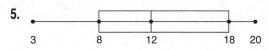

6.

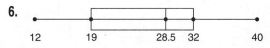

7.

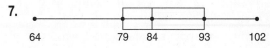

8.

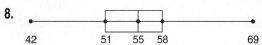

9. Answers vary.

■ **Lesson 5.4**

1.

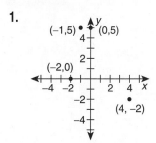

2.

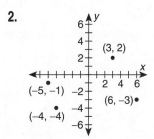

3.

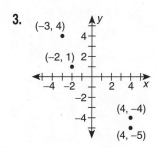

4.

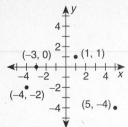

(−3, 0) (1, 1)
(−4, −2)
(5, −4)

5. On January 21 the high temperature was 4° F.
On the 22nd the high temperature was −7° F.
On the 23rd the high temperature was 2° F.
On the 24th the high temperature was 0° F.
And on the 25th the high temperature was 3° F.

6. 3° F

7.

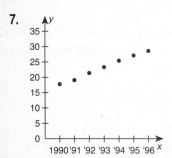

Answers vary.

8.

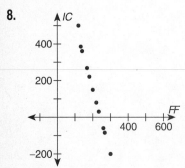

9. Answers vary.   **10.** About $325 profit

11. About $270 profit

■ **Lesson 5.5**

1.

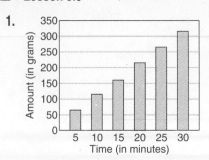

or

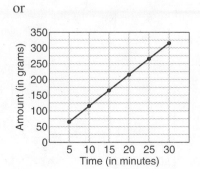

$y = 10x + 15$

2.

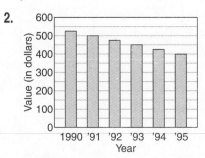

or

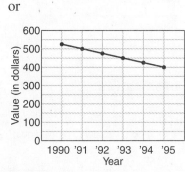

$y = -25(x - 1990) + 525$

3.

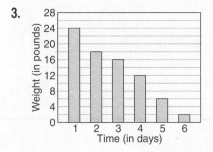

or

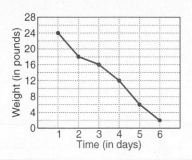

No pattern

4.

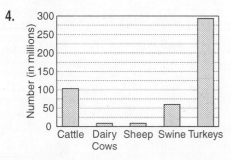

The number of chickens is so large that it would not fit in well with the given data.

5.

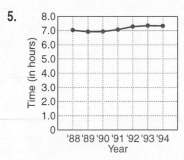

The time of TV usage seems to relatively constant.

6.

Country	Total Medals Awarded
United States	☺ ☺ ☺ ☺ ☺ ☺ ☺ ☺ ☺ (
Germany	☺ ☺ ☺ ☺ ☺ ☺ ☺ (
Russia	☺ ☺ ☺ ☺ ☺ ☺ (
China	☺ ☺ ☺ ☺ ☺
Australia	☺ ☺ ☺ ☺ (
France	☺ ☺ ☺ ☺ (
Italy	☺ ☺ ☺ (
South Korea	☺ ☺ (
Cuba	☺ ☺ (
Ukraine	☺ ☺ (☺ = 10 medals

Three to four countries appear to win the most medals. The remaining countries are relatively equal.

■ Lesson 5.6

1. Appears to be about 3 times as high

2. Rogun is about 160 feet higher than Chicoasen.

3. The scale starts at 800 feet.

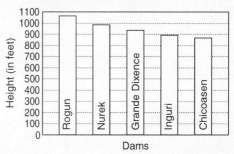

4. The two separate graphs are misleading because the graphs have different scales.

5. The graphs have different scales, making the data appear to be approximately the same for each year.

6.

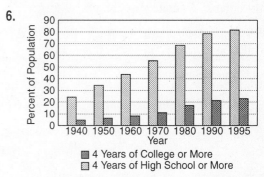

Yes, you could compare the two lines on the same graph.

■ Lesson 5.7

1. c   **2.** a   **3.** b   **4.** 0.21   **5.** 0.40

6. 0.60   **7.** 0.55   **8.** 0.10   **9.** 0.10   **10.** 0.90

■ Lesson 6.1

1. Yes, same units of measure

2. No, different units of measure

3. No, different units of measure

4. Yes, same units of measures

5. $\dfrac{30 \text{ inches}}{96 \text{ inches}} = \dfrac{5}{16}$ **6.** $\dfrac{32 \text{ ounces}}{18 \text{ ounces}} = \dfrac{16}{9}$

7. $\dfrac{48 \text{ hours}}{15 \text{ hours}} = \dfrac{16}{5}$ **8.** $\dfrac{12 \text{ pints}}{32 \text{ pints}} = \dfrac{3}{8}$

9. $\dfrac{24 \text{ in.}}{28 \text{ in.}} = \dfrac{6}{7}$ **10.** $\dfrac{12 \text{ cm}}{48 \text{ cm}} = \dfrac{1}{4}$

11. $\dfrac{52 \text{ cm}}{60 \text{ cm}} = \dfrac{13}{15}$ **12.** $\dfrac{90 \text{ min}}{480 \text{ min}} = \dfrac{3}{16}$

13. $\dfrac{300 \text{ mL}}{2000 \text{ mL}} = \dfrac{3}{20}$

■ **Lesson 6.2**

1. $\frac{3}{8}$; ratio   2. $\frac{16}{9}$; ratio

3. $\frac{3 \text{ feet}}{1 \text{ second}}$; rate   4. $\frac{12 \text{ points}}{1 \text{ game}}$; rate

5. $\frac{\frac{1}{15} \text{ mile}}{1 \text{ minute}}$ or $\frac{4 \text{ miles}}{1 \text{ hour}}$ 6. $\frac{\$5.75}{1 \text{ lawn}}$

7. $\frac{\$10.50}{1 \text{ page}}$ 8. $\frac{5000 \text{ calculations}}{1 \text{ second}}$

9. The 24-oz can; because it costs $0.044 per oz while the 20-oz can costs $0.045 per oz.

10. The 25-lb crate; because it costs $0.64 per lb while the 20-lb crate costs $0.68 per lb.

11. The 32-oz jar; because it costs $0.064 per oz while the $27\frac{1}{2}$-oz jar costs $0.069 per oz.

12. 32.3 transplants per day

13. 1.73 people to a car

■ **Lesson 6.3**

1. True   2. False   3. True

4. $\frac{e}{8} = \frac{4}{16}$; $e = 2$ 5. $\frac{y}{20} = \frac{18}{72}$; $y = 5$

6. $\frac{75}{15} = \frac{w}{5}$; $w = 25$ 7. $\frac{80}{5} = \frac{t}{3}$; $t = 48$

8. 12   9. 14   10. 50   11. 10

12. 2   13. 81   14. 26 gal   15. 2 hr

■ **Lesson 6.4**

1. True   2. True   3. True   4. False

5. False   6. True   7. 18   8. 12.5

9. 175   10. 48   11. 62.5   12. 11.4

12. 9.5   14. 8   15. $\frac{8 \text{ in.}}{24 \text{ in.}} = \frac{1}{3} = \frac{12 \text{ in.}}{36 \text{ in.}}$

16. $\frac{14 \text{ cm}}{35 \text{ cm}} = \frac{2}{5} = \frac{4 \text{ cm}}{10 \text{ cm}}$ 17. 6.86

18. 24.55   19. 14.25   20. 15.83

■ **Lesson 6.5**

1. c; 7.5 cups   2. b; 137.5 miles

3. $\frac{24 \text{ lb}}{1750 \text{ sq ft}} = \frac{x \text{ lb}}{6562.5 \text{ sq ft}}$; 90 lb

4. $\frac{2 \text{ grams}}{5 \text{ liters}} = \frac{x \text{ grams}}{28 \text{ liters}}$; 11.2 grams

5. $\frac{9 \text{ votes}}{16 \text{ people}} = \frac{x \text{ votes}}{30,000 \text{ people}}$; 16,875 votes

6. $\frac{36 \text{ min}}{750 \text{ gal}} = \frac{x \text{ min}}{250 \text{ gal}}$; 12 min

■ **Lesson 6.6**

1. $\angle D = \angle M$, $\angle E = \angle O$, $\angle F = \angle N$,
$\frac{DE}{OM} = \frac{24}{60} = \frac{2}{5}$, $\frac{DF}{MN} = \frac{10}{25} = \frac{2}{5}$, $\frac{EF}{ON} = \frac{26}{65} = \frac{2}{5}$

2. All anlges measure 90°
$\frac{PQ}{EF} = \frac{9}{15} = \frac{3}{5}$, $\frac{WV}{GH} = \frac{12}{20} = \frac{3}{5}$, $\frac{QR}{ED} = \frac{12}{20} = \frac{3}{5}$,
$\frac{UV}{AH} = \frac{18}{30} = \frac{3}{5}$, $\frac{PW}{FG} = \frac{12}{20} = \frac{3}{5}$, $\frac{ST}{BC} = \frac{18}{30} = \frac{3}{5}$,
$\frac{RS}{DC} = \frac{12}{20} = \frac{3}{5}$, $\frac{UT}{AB} = \frac{33}{55} = \frac{3}{5}$

3. $\angle K = 52°$, $ML = 15$, $\angle R = 28°$, $RP = 34$

4. $EH = 22.5$

5. $\angle X = 120°$, $\angle Z = 60°$, $WZ = 12$, $\angle N = 60°$, $\angle P = 120°$, $PO = 6$, $MN = 24$, $MP = 18$

6. $\angle D = 51°$, $DF = 20$, $GI = 30$, $\angle G = 39°$

7. $\frac{4 \text{ ft}}{5 \text{ ft}} = \frac{20 \text{ ft}}{x \text{ ft}}$; 25 ft

■ **Lesson 6.7**

1. 150 mi   2. 125 mi   3. 18.75 mi

4. 430 mi   5. 60 ft   6. 44 m

7. About 360 mi   8. About 450 mi

9. About 475 mi   10. About 180 mi

11. About 810 mi

12. 31 square feet;

Lesson 7.1

1. $0.1, \frac{1}{10}$ 2. $0.3, \frac{3}{10}$ 3. $0.75, \frac{3}{4}$

4. $0.95, \frac{19}{20}$ 5. $\frac{84}{100}, 84\%$ 6. $\frac{7}{100}, 7\%$

7. $\frac{1.5}{100}, 1.5\%$ 8. $\frac{60}{100}, 60\%$ 9. 28%

10. 40% 11. 62.5% 12. 85%

13. 52% 14. 70% 15. 50%

16. $\frac{38}{100}$, the other numbers in the list all represent 76%.

17. $\frac{28}{95}$, the other numbers in the list all represent 26.7%.

18. Bored with arrangement: 36%
Redecorating: 16%
Moving to new residence: 19%
Purchased new furniture: 15%
Other: 14%

Lesson 7.2

1. 40%, 100 marbles   2. 80%, 20 quarters

3. 72%, 720 pencils   4. 105 miles

5. 8 students   6. $25   7. 0.15, 18

8. 0.78, 273   9. 0.12, 30   10. 0.98, 490

11. 0.02, 10   12. 0.64, 32   13. 0.84, 357

14. 0.55, 11   15. 84.5   16. 9

17. 42 in.   18. 81 employees

Lesson 7.3

1. $1.5, \frac{3}{2}$ 2. $0.002, \frac{1}{500}$ 3. $0.00875, \frac{7}{800}$

4. $3.25, \frac{13}{4}$ 5. 125%   6. 750%

7. $\frac{2}{5}\%$ or 0.4%   8. $\frac{1}{4}\%$ or 0.25%   9. 182%

10. 535%   12. $\frac{1}{20}\%$ or 0.05%

12. $\frac{14}{25}\%$ or 0.56%   13. $300   14. 900 coins

15. 20 mi   16. =   17. <   18. <   19. =

20. >   21. <   22. less than 60 bulbs

23. 9250 members

Lesson 7.4

1. 91,800   2. 1120   3. $540

4. 9900 voters   5. 28   6. 410   7. 28%

8. 15%   9. 600   10. 460   11. 1000

12. 8   13. 70%   14. 16 oz   15. $3250

Lesson 7.5

1. 56 students   2. 4 more

3. 3 times as many

4.
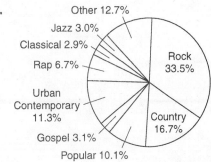

5.
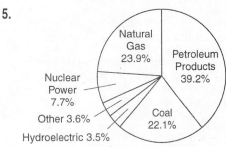

6.
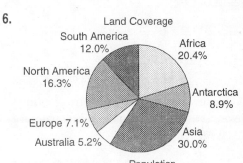

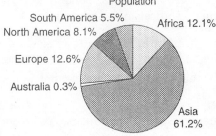

7. 17,192,627 sq mi

8. About 439,051,671 people

Lesson 7.6

1. $30   2. $60   3. $80   4. $120

5. $960   6. $1200   7. $1440   8. $1920

9. $20, $520   10. $90, $1590

11. $1056.25, $7556.25   12. $1150, $12,650

13. $127.50, $4627.50   14. $3200, $19,200

15. 6.5%   **16.** 18 months

■ **Lesson 7.7**

1. 50% increase   **2.** 75% increase

3. 35% decrease   **4.** 15% decrease

5. 65% increase   **6.** 25% increase

7. 40% increase   **8.** 95% decrease

9. 2.0% increase   **10.** 36.8% increase

11. 50.1% increase   **12.** 4.7% decrease

13. 8.0% decrease   **14.** 76.2% decrease

15. 92.2% increase

■ **Lesson 8.1**

1. 40°   **2.** 140°   **3.** 140°   **4.** 40°

5. corresponding or vertical   **6.** vertical

7. parallel   **8.** intersecting

9. $\angle 2 \cong \angle 8 \cong \angle 6 \cong \angle 4$

10. $\angle 2 \cong \angle 3$

11. $\angle 2 \cong \angle 3 \cong \angle 6 \cong \angle 8 \cong \angle 9 \cong \angle 11$
$\cong \angle 14 \cong \angle 16$

12. $\angle b = 90°$, $\angle a = 90°$; $\angle b$ is a vertical angle to a 90° angle and $\angle a$ and $\angle b$ are corresponding angles. $\angle c = 30°$; the sum of complementary angles is 90°.

13. $\angle a = 85°$, $\angle b = 85°$; corresponding angles are congruent, vertical angles are congruent.

14. $\angle a = 75°$, $\angle b = 75°$, $\angle c = 30°$; vertical angles are congruent and sum of the angles of triangle is 180°. $\angle d = 105°$; the sum of supplementary angles is 180°.

15. Interstates 77 and 79, and Interstates 78 and 80

16. $\angle a = 70°$, $\angle b = 55°$, $\angle c = 70°$, $\angle d = 55°$, $\angle e = 55°$

■ **Lesson 8.2**

1. 5 units right and 3 units down

2. 4 units right and 4 units up

3. 6 units left and 4 units down

4. A' (1, −2), B' (3, −6), C' (−5, −5)

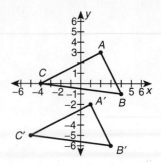

5. J' (0, 0), K' (4, 0), L' (6, 3), M' (−2, 3)

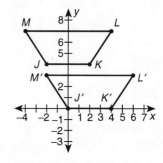

6. 4 units left and 2 units up

7. 2 units right and 1 unit down

8. (1, 1)A, (3, −2)N, (−1, −1)G, (2, −4)E, (−2, 1)L; ANGEL

9. Answers vary.

■ **Lesson 8.3**

1. 75.36 ft   **2.** 50.24 cm   **3.** 31.4 in.

4. b   **5.** c   **6.** a   **7.** 15 in.   **8.** 19 yd

9. 12 cm   **10.** 38.3 in.   **11.** 6.9 in.

12. 8.8 ft   **13.** 44.6 in.   **14.** 62.8 mi

■ **Lesson 8.4**

1. 162 sq m   **2.** 36 sq cm   **3.** 480 sq in.

4.–6. Answers vary.   **7.** 30 in.   **8.** 15 cm

9. $27\frac{1}{2}$ yd

10.

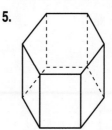

Area = $2(\frac{1}{2})(3)(11) + (5)(11)$

     = 33 + 55 = 88 sq units

Area = (8)(11) = 88 sq units

11. Estimates vary; actual area: 69,686 sq mi

12. Estimates vary; actual area: 33,215 sq mi

■ **Lesson 8.5**

1. It is; height: 60 cm, area: 3600 sq cm

2. It is not.

3. It is; height: 90 yd, area: 4860 sq yd

4. 60 sq cm   **5.** 141.75 sq in.   **6.** 364 sq cm

7. 34,375 sq yd   **8.** 9 cm   **9.** 30 yd

10. 24 m   **11.** 1176 sq cm   **12.** 576 sq cm

13. 176 sq in.   **14.** 1800 sq ft

■ **Lesson 8.6**

1. 116.84 sq in.   **2.** 3.80 sq in.

3. 6.15 sq ft   **4.** 633.15 sq in.

5. 50.24 sq ft; 25.12 ft

6. 1017.36 sq cm, 113.04 cm

7. 254.34 sq yd, 56.52 yd

8. 5538.96 sq km, 263.76 km

9. 123.84 sq in.   **10.** 43.96 sq cm

11. 42.39 sq ft

12. radius: 15.3 in., area: 735.0 sq in.

13. radius: 9.2 cm, area: 265.8 sq cm

14. radius: 6 cm, area: 113.0 sq cm

15. 3925 sq ft   **16.** radius: 4.5 ft, area: 63.6 sq ft

■ **Lesson 8.7**

1. 6   **2.** 12   **3.** 23   **4.** 8.4   **5.** 4.9

6. 3.74   **7.** 8.94   **8.** 7.52

9. 10.1 ft, $\sqrt{102.01} = 10.1$

10. 4.8 cm; the area of one square is $\frac{1}{6}$ of the total area. $138.24 \div 6 = 23.04$, $\sqrt{23.04} = 4.8$

11. 18.4 in.; the area is $\frac{1}{2}$ of the area of the square. $169.28 \cdot 2 = 338.56$, $\sqrt{338.56} = 18.4$

12.–19. Estimates vary.

12. 2.83   **13.** 4.47   **14.** 9.22   **15.** 13.04

16. 6.93   **17.** 8.25   **18.** 19.75   **19.** 25.10

20. 625 sq ft

■ **Lesson 8.8**

1. Acute   **2.** Right, p **3.** Right, x **4.** 25 ft

5. 30.6 cm   **6.** 62.5 in.   **7.** 36.06   **8.** 96.18

9. 123.22   **10.** 24 cm   **11.** 72 ft

12. 63 in.   **13.** 180.3 mi   **14.** About 43 yd

■ **Lesson 9.1**

1. Yes, square pyramid

2. Yes, rectangular prism

3. No   **4.** Yes, hexagonal prism

5.

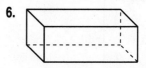

hexagonal prism

6.

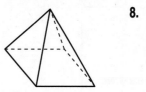

rectangular prism

7.   **8.**

square pyramid   cube

9.   **10.**

octagonal pyramid   pentagonal prism

11. a. hexagonal prism   **b.** 8
　　c. 18   **d.** 12

12. a. triangular prism   **b.** 5
　　c. 9   **d.** 6

13. a. octagonal prism   **b.** 10
　　c. 24   **d.** 16

■ **Lesson 9.2**

1. b; 52 sq cm   2. a; 66 sq cm

3. c; 32 sq cm   4. 41.5 sq in.

5. 2058 sq cm   6. 85.125 sq in.

7. 432 sq in.   8. 256 sq cm

9. 6000 sq cm   10. 54 sq in.   11. 126 sq in.

■ **Lesson 9.3**

1. Yes   2. No   3. Yes   4. Yes

5. 1381.6 sq in.   6. 2009.6 sq cm

7. 580.3 sq in.   8. d, 3736.6 sq mm

9. a, 56.52, sq in.   10. b, 239.14 sq in.

11. c, 596.6 sq cm

12. a. 879.2 sq in.   **b.** 698.5 sq in.
　　c. 659.4 sq in.

■ **Lesson 9.4**

1. a   2. c   3. b

4.
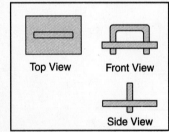

5.
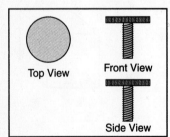

6.
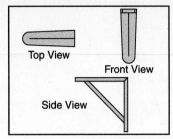

7. rectangular prism   8. cylinder

9. triangular prism   10. b   11. c   12. a

■ **Lesson 9.5**

1. 840 cu in.   2. 350 cu cm   3. 8 cu ft

4. 192 cu ft   5. 1759.5 cu cm

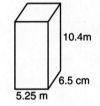

6. 354.9 cu m   7. $277\frac{1}{3}$ cu yd

8. 232 sq in.; 160 cu in.

9. 268.4 sq cm; 240 cu cm

10. 3232 sq ft; 11,520 cu ft   11. $x = 12$ cm

12. $x = \frac{1}{2}$ ft or 6 in.   13. $x = 6.5$ cm

14. 118.8 minutes or 118 minutes 48 seconds

■ **Lesson 9.6**

1. 1356.48 in.^{3} 2. 1808.64 cm^3

3. 62.8 mm^3 4. 1.57 ft^3 or 2712.96 in.^{3}

5. $h = 13$ in.   6. $h = 8$ cm   7. $r = 7$ in.

8. $r = 15$ m

9. A cylinder with radius of 3.5 in. and a height
of 2 in.; the radius of the cylinder would be one
half the width of the box and the height the
same as the box; $V = 76.93$ in.^{3}; extra space =
119.07 in.^{3}.

10. Approximately 1973.59 lb (1968.59 lb of sand)

11. 4823.04 cubic ft   12. 452.16 cubic in.

■ **Lesson 9.7**

1. Yes, 1 to 3   **2.** No   **3.** 175 cm; 30 cm

4. 90 ft; 16 cm   **5.** $x = 18$ m, $y = 32$ m

6. $x = 9.6$ ft, $y = 12.5$ ft

7.

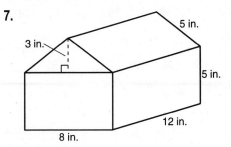

5 in.
3 in.
5 in.
12 in.
8 in.

8. 11.5 ft by 19 ft by 7 ft

■ **Lesson 10.1**

1. ◄─┼─┼─┼─┼─┼─┼─┼─┼─┼─┼─┼─●─┼─►
    −6 −5 −4 −3 −2 −1 0 1 2 3 4 5 6

2. ◄─┼─┼─●─┼─┼─┼─┼─┼─●─┼─┼─┼─►
    −6 −5 −4 −3 −2 −1 0 1 2 3 4 5 6

3. ◄─┼─┼─┼─┼─┼─┼─┼─┼─┼─┼─┼─┼─┼─●─┼─►
    −8 −7 −6 −5 −4 −3 −2 −1 0 1 2 3 4 5 6 7 8

4. ◄●─┼─┼─┼─┼─┼─┼─┼─┼─┼─┼─●►
    −10 −8 −6 −4 −2 0 2 4 6 8 10

5. $|4.5| = 4.5$ **6.** $|-4| = 4$ **7.** $|2.5| = 2.5$

8. $|-1.5| = 1.5$ **9.** 8   **10.** 5   **11.** 8

12. 5.2   **13.** 8.2   **14.** 1.6   **15.** 0.5

16. 15   **17.** >   **18.** <   **19.** =   **20.** <

21. <   **22.** <

23. $|7.25 - 9| = |-1.75| = 1.75$ hours

24. $|9.75 - 7| = |2.75| = 2.75$ hours

25. $|9.25 - 8| = |1.25| = 1.25$ hours

26. American history

■ **Lesson 10.2**

1. Negative, −3   **2.** Negative, −27

3. Zero, 0   **4.** Positive, 4   **5.** 7

6. −18   **7.** 3   **8.** 0   **9.** −20   **10.** −38

11. −13   **12.** 6   **13.** 33   **14.** −4

15. 36   **16.** 27   **17.** −12   **18.** −30

19. −7   **20.** −3   **21.** 2

22.–25. Answers vary.   **26.** $15

■ **Lesson 10.3**

1. $5 + (-16); -11$ **2.** $0 + (-15); -15$

3. $-5 + (-1); -6$ **4.** $-4 + (-18); -22$

5. $0 + 10; 10$ **6.** $-15 + 3; -12$

7. $25 + 12; 37$ **8.** $-1 + 1; 0$

9. −13   **10.** −3   **11.** −24   **12.** −20

13. 22   **14.** 25   **15.** −34   **16.** 35

17. −1, −9   **18.** 10, 18   **19.** −11, −3

20. 3, 11   **21.** b, −9   **22.** c, −39   **23.** a, 39

■ **Lesson 10.4**

1.

x	−5	−3	−1	1	3
y	0	−2	−4	−6	−8

2.

x	8	4	0	−4	−8
y	4	0	−4	−8	−12

3.

x	−4	−2	0	2	4
y	9	7	5	3	1

4. (−2, −5), (−1, −4), (0, −3), (1, −2), (2, −1)

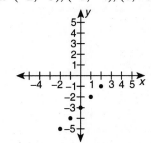

For each increase of 1 in the x-value, the y-value increases by 1.

5. (−2, 0), (−1, −1), (0, −2), (1, −3), (2, −4)

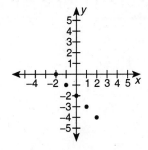

For each increase of 1 in the x-value, the y-value decreases by 1.

6. (−2, 6), (−1, 5), (0, 4), (1, 3), (2, 2)

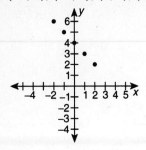

For each increase of 1 in the *x*-value,
the *y*-value decreases by 1.

7.

x	−4	−3	−2	−1	0	1	2	3	4
y	−3	−2	−1	0	1	2	3	4	5

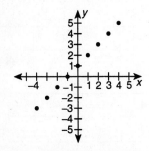

For each increase of 1 in the *x*-value,
the *y*-value increases by 1.

8.

x	−4	−3	−2	−1	0	1	2	3	4
y	−5	−4	−3	−2	−1	0	1	2	3

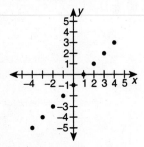

For each increase of 1 in the *x*-value,
the *y*-value increases by 1.

9.

x	−4	−3	−2	−1	0	1	2	3	4
y	0	−1	−2	−3	−4	−5	−6	−7	−8

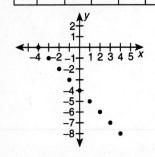

For each increase of 1 in the *x*-value,
the *y*-value decreases by 1.

10. b   **11.** c   **12.** a

■ **Lesson 10.5**

1. Zero   **2.** Positive   **3.** Positive

4. Negative   **5.** Positive   **6.** Negative

7. 36   **8.** −40   **9.** 0   **10.** 10   **11.** −24

12. 0   **13.** 8   **14.** 5   **15.** −3   **16.** −4

17. −2   **18.** 3   **19.** −190.32   **20.** −144

21. 7215   **22.** 36   **23.** $-\frac{1}{4}$ or -0.25

24. −48

25. $C = (F - 32) \times \frac{5}{9}$

F	5	23	50	68	86	95	104
C	−15	−5	10	20	30	35	40

■ **Lesson 10.6**

1. Negative   **2.** Negative   **3.** Positive

4. Positive   **5.** −5   **6.** 5   **7.** −12

8. 0   **9.** −4   **10.** 8   **11.** −3   **12.** −6

13. −2 yards   **14.** 35 students   **15.** −31 feet

16. −5, 13   **17.** 1, 19   **18.** −1, 1   **19.** 3, −3

20. −7   **21.** 18   **22.** −5   **23.** −3° F

■ **Lesson 10.7**

1. 9   **2.** −25   **3.** 8   **4.** 48   **5.** −60

6. 9   **7.** −17   **8.** −9

9.

x	−3	−2	−1	0	1	2	3
y	36	16	4	0	4	16	36

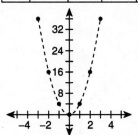

The points form a U-shape that opens up.

10.

x	−3	−2	−1	0	1	2	3
y	11	6	3	2	3	6	11

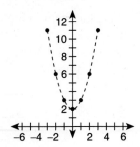

The points form a U-shape that opens up.

11.

x	−3	−2	−1	0	1	2	3
y	−5	0	3	4	3	0	−5

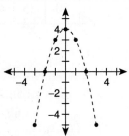

The points form a U-shape that opens down.

12.

x	−3	−2	−1	0	1	2	3
y	−18	−8	−2	0	−2	−8	−18

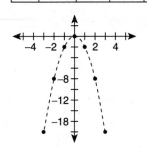

The points form a U-shape that opens down.

13. > **14.** < **15.** > **16.** = **17.** > **18.** <

19. 972 **20.** −728 **21.** −972 **22.** −104

23.

x	0	1	2	3	4	5	6	7
y	4	84	132	148	132	84	4	−106

The object rises to a maximum height of 148 feet then falls. It strikes the ground between 6 and 7 seconds.

■ **Lesson 10.8**

1. 10,000 **2.** $\dfrac{1}{100,000,000}$

3. 1,000,000,000 **4.** $\dfrac{1}{1,000,000,000,000}$

5. 8.5×10^5 **6.** 1.952×10^7

7. 2.53×10^{-2} **8.** 8.5×10^{-5}

9. 5.48×10^{11} **10.** 9.84×10^{-11}

11. 5.88×10^{12} **12.** 6.31×10^7

13. 9.0×10^{-30} **14.** < **15.** > **16.** <

17. = **18.** a **19.** b

■ **Lesson 11.1**

1. Both parents are red. The probability of red is $\frac{4}{4}$. The probability of white is $\frac{0}{4}$.

	R	r
R	RR	Rr
R	RR	Rr

2. Both parents are red. The probability of red is $\frac{3}{4}$. The probability of white is $\frac{1}{4}$.

	R	r
r	rR	rr
R	RR	Rr

3. One parent is red and one is white. The probability of red is $\frac{2}{4}$. The probability of white is $\frac{2}{4}$.

	r	R
r	rr	rR
r	rr	rR

4. One parent is red and one is white. The probability of red is $\frac{4}{4}$. The probability of white is $\frac{0}{4}$.

	R	R
r	rR	rR
r	rR	rR

5. Red: 3 pieces, Yellow: 1 piece, Blue: 8 pieces, Green: 6 pieces

6. $\frac{6}{36} = \frac{1}{6}$

	1	2	3	4	5	6
1	2	3	4	5	6	7
2	3	4	5	6	7	8
3	4	5	6	7	8	9
4	5	6	7	8	9	10
5	6	7	8	9	10	11
6	7	8	9	10	11	12

7. $\frac{1}{8}$ **8.** $\frac{60}{500} = \frac{3}{25}$ **9.** $\frac{440}{500} = \frac{22}{25}$ **10.** $\frac{120}{500} = \frac{6}{25}$

■ **Lesson 11.2**

1. Answers vary.

2. 24;

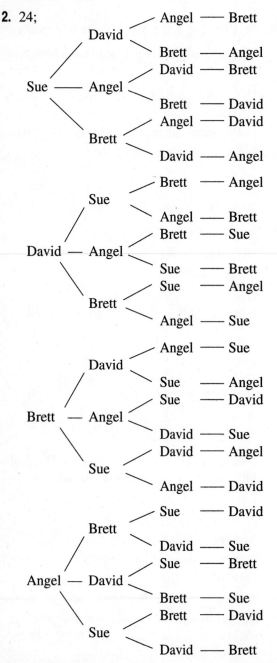

3. $100, \frac{1}{100}$ **4.** 720   **5.** $\frac{1}{720}$

6. 720   **7.** 3600

8. Predictions vary. Since the number of entrees is half the original number, the total number of meals possible should be one half the total before the 5 entrees were eliminated. 1800 different meals

■ **Lesson 11.3**

1. 24   **2.** 362,880   **3.** 720   **4.** 39,916,800

5. 6 permutations

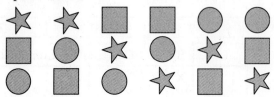

6. 24 permutations

b = baseball   f = football
bb = basketball   s = soccerball

b	f	bb	s		f	bb	s	b
b	f	s	bb		f	bb	b	s
b	bb	s	f		f	b	bb	s
b	bb	f	s		f	b	s	bb
b	s	bb	f		f	s	b	bb
b	s	f	bb		f	s	bb	b
s	b	f	bb		bb	s	f	b
s	b	bb	f		bb	s	b	f
s	f	bb	b		bb	f	b	s
s	f	b	bb		bb	f	s	b
s	bb	f	b		bb	b	f	s
s	bb	b	f		bb	b	s	f

7. 6, <u>RAT</u>, RTA, <u>TAR</u>, TRA, <u>ART</u>, ATR; 3 are words.

8. 24, <u>POST</u>, <u>POTS</u>, PSTO, PSOT, PTSO, PTOS, OSTP, OSPT, OTSP, OTPS, <u>OPTS</u>, OPST, TOSP, <u>TOPS</u>, TPSO, TPOS, TSPO, TSOP, SOPT, SOTP, <u>STOP</u>, STPO, <u>SPOT</u>, SPTO; 6 are words.

9. $\frac{1}{6!} = \frac{1}{720}$ **10.** $5! = 120; \frac{1}{5!} = \frac{1}{120}$

11. $\frac{1}{7!} = \frac{1}{5040}$ **12.** $\frac{1}{4!} = \frac{1}{24}$

Lesson 11.4

1.

	A	B	C	D	E	Combination
1	X	X				AB
2	X		X			AC
3	X			X		AD
4	X				X	AE
5		X	X			BC
6		X		X		BD
7		X			X	BE
8			X	X		CD
9			X		X	CE
10				X	X	DE

2.

	A	B	C	D	E	F	Combination
1	X	X	X				ABC
2	X	X		X			ABD
3	X	X			X		ABE
4	X	X				X	ABF
5	X		X	X			ACD
6	X		X		X		ACE
7	X		X			X	ACF
8	X			X	X		ADE
9	X			X		X	ADF
10	X				X	X	AEF
11		X	X	X			BCD
12		X	X		X		BCE
13		X	X			X	BCF
14		X		X	X		BDE
15		X		X		X	BDF
16		X			X	X	BEF
17			X	X	X		CDE
18			X	X		X	CDF
19			X		X	X	CEF
20				X	X	X	DEF

3.

	A	B	C	D	E	Combination
1	X	X	X	X		ABCD
2	X	X	X		X	ABCE
3	X	X		X	X	ABDE
4	X		X	X	X	ACDE
5		X	X	X	X	BCDE

4. ★ ■
★ ●
★ ●
■ ●

5. r, b, g
r, b, w
b, g, w
r, g, w

---

6. 02, 04, 06, 24, 26, 46

7. 10; ABC, ABD, ABE, ACD, ACE, ADE, BCD, BCE, BDE, CDE

8. 30 games   **9.** permutations, $9! = 362,880$

10. combinations, 28

11. combinations, $\frac{1}{45} \approx 0.02$

12. combinations, $\frac{1}{35} \approx 0.03$

Lesson 11.5

1. No, yellow   **2.** Yes   **3.** No, purple

4. $\frac{1}{2} \cdot 2 + \frac{1}{3} \cdot 3 + \frac{1}{6} \cdot 6 = 3$ points

5. $\frac{3}{4} \cdot 0 + \frac{1}{4} \cdot 5 = \frac{5}{4}$ points

6. $\frac{1}{8} \cdot 10 + \frac{3}{8} \cdot 5 + \frac{3}{8} \cdot 1 + \frac{1}{8} \cdot 0 = \frac{7}{2}$ points

7. The game is fair. Ginger and David both have expected value of $\frac{10}{3}$ points.

8. The game is not fair. Brett's expected value is $\frac{13}{2}$ points. Sue's expected value is $\frac{55}{8}$ points. Sue is most likely going to win.

Lesson 11.6

1. About 188 times   **2.** About 250 times

3. About 167 times   **4.** $\frac{4.1}{57.4} \approx 0.07$

5. About 82 times   **6.** Answers vary.

7. Points vary.   **8.** $\frac{1}{2} \cdot 60 = 30$ times

9.

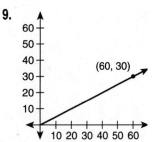

10. Number of points above and below the line vary.

Lesson 11.7

1. 0.36   **2.** 0.12   **3.** 0.48   **4.** 0.08

5. These sets overlap because some people like country music but not rock music, some people like rock music but not country music, and some people like both.

6. These sets are disjoint because one cannot enjoy riding a bike and also not enjoy riding a bike.

7. The set of people who enjoy jogging is a subset of people who enjoy exercising.

8. These subsets overlap because some people eat pizza with pepperoni but not sausage and some people eat pizza with sausage but not pepperoni and some people eat pizza with both. The people who eat pizza with pepperoni and/or sausage is a subset of the people who eat pizza.

9.–13.

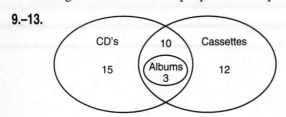

9. $\frac{15}{40} \approx 0.38$ **10.** $\frac{12}{40} = 0.30$ **11.** $\frac{0}{40} = 0$

12. $\frac{10}{40} = 0.25$ **13.** $\frac{3}{40} \approx 0.08$

■ Lesson 12.1

1. Add 8   **2.** Subtract –5   **3.** Divide by 2

4. Multiply by –6   **5.** –13   **6.** 25   **7.** 6

8. –10   **9.** 14   **10.** 1   **11.** 3   **12.** –48

13.

+8

| e | –2 |

$e = -10$

14.

–15

| w | 3 |

$w = 18$

15.

× (–12)

| r | –48 |

$r = 4$

16.

– (–14)

| s | 26 |

$s = 12$

17.

÷ 9

| j | –2 |

$j = -18$

18.

× 15

| q | –45 |

$q = -3$

19. $x - (-6) = -1; x = -7$

20. $x \cdot 2.6 = -7.8; x = -3$

21. $\frac{x}{-5} = -2.1; x = 10.5$

22. $x + 3.24 = 0.2; x = -3.04$

■ Lesson 12.2

1. No   **2.** No   **3.** Yes   **4.** $e - 15 = 20; 35$

5. $-20 = w + 12; -32$ **6.** $t + 10 = 20; 10$

7. $x + 7 + 6 + 7 = 22; 2$

8. $x + 15 + 90 = 180; 75$

9. $x + 16 + 10 = 40; 14$

10. $\frac{9}{10}$ **11.** –17.8   **12.** $-\frac{17}{8}$

13. $1.2 + x = 4.5; x = 3.3$ inches

14. $x - 24.99 = 74.96; \$99.95$

■ Lesson 12.3

1. Negative; –5   **2.** Positive; 4

3. Positive; 8   **4.** Negative; $-\frac{15}{2}$ **5.** $\frac{46}{3}$

6. $\frac{51}{5}$ **7.** $-\frac{13}{6}$ **8.** $\frac{32}{3}$ **9.** –4.8   **10.** 5

11. –0.4   **12.** 0.6   **13.** 12   **14.** –15

15. 0   **16.** –2.4   **17.** $\frac{5}{4}$ **18.** –6   **19.** 3

20. 3.8   **21.** $-4x = 24; -6$

22. $-32 = 6.4x; -5$ **23.** $-7x = -119; 17$

24. $203 = 58t; 3.5$ hours

■ Lesson 12.4

1. Negative   **2.** Positive   **3.** Negative

4. Positive   **5.** 30   **6.** 18   **7.** –45

8. 3   **9.** $\frac{1}{2}$ **10.** –26.25   **11.** –65.6

12. 30.8   **13.** 20.16

14. $\frac{x}{8} = 12$ or $\frac{x}{12} = 8$; 96 sq cm

15. $\frac{x}{9} = 10$ or $\frac{x}{10} = 9$; 90 sq in.

16. $\frac{x}{2} = 6$ or $\frac{x}{6} = 2$ or $\frac{x}{3} = 4$ or $\frac{x}{4} = 3$; 12 sq mi

17. $\frac{x}{340.5} = \frac{4}{1}$; 1362 feet

■ Lesson 12.5

1. Subtract 5 from both sides of the equation.

2. Add 15 to both sides of the equation.

3. Add 5 to both sides of the equation.

4. $3x + 2 = 17; 5$ **5.** $-2x - 5 = 11; -8$

6. $5x - 1 = -4; -\frac{3}{5}$ **7.** –4   **8.** 2

9. 12   **10.** $\frac{3}{2}$ **11.** 0   **12.** 10   **13.** 1

14. 1.65   **15.** $x = 13; 25°, 65°, 90°$

16. $x = 16; 90°, 90°, 121°, 59°$

17. Beachbum's: $2x + 16 = 40$; $x = 12$ hours
Waverunner's: $3x + 10 = 40$; $x = 10$ hours
Beachbum's is the better bargain if you want to
rent the bike as long as possible.

■ **Lesson 12.6**

1.

Input, x	1	2	3	4	5	6
Output, y	8	11	14	17	20	23

2.

Input, x	1	2	3	4	5	6
Output, y	$-\frac{1}{2}$	0	$\frac{1}{2}$	1	$\frac{3}{2}$	2

3.

Input, x	1	2	3	4	5	6
Output, y	0	−5	−10	−15	−20	−25

4.

Input, x	1	2	3	4	5	6
Output, y	12	16	20	24	28	32

5. $y = 2x - 1$ **6.** $y = -x + 3$

7. $y = 5x - 1$ **8.** $y = 0.5x + 1$

9.

Input, t	1	2	3	4	5	6
Output, n	50	100	150	200	250	300

10. $n = 50t$

11.

Input, n	10	20	30	40	50
Output, c	20	35	50	65	80

12. $c = 1.5n + 5$